ANDREW MARTIN

Interior Design Review Volume 19

teNeues

Timeless and classic are two words that designers love to use to describe their work. It's only natural that everybody wants their work to stand the test of time. In fact, timeless and classic are virtually impossible aspirations.

Even the greatest of designers are shaped by the times they live in. When you review the work of Billy Baldwin, who was perhaps the most influential of American post war decorators, it's obvious that he was working in the 1950's. David Hicks who still resides at the top of Mount Olympus in the interior design pantheon, is defined by the quintessential zing of the 60's and 70's.

And it was ever thus. Everybody can recognise the difference between Chippendale and Empire furniture, even though the high watermark of each is only separated by a few years. Thomas Chippendale's designs dominated the second half of the 18th century. The greatest aristocratic families beat a path to his door.

However by 1804 Chippendale was declared bankrupt and reduced to the ignominy of a fire sale of his stock. Design had moved on. However, it's worth pointing out that in 1992, a pair of Chippendale mirrors (originally made for Harewood House in 1775 for £40) fetched £319,000 and in 2010 the Harrington Commode was auctioned by Sotheby's for almost £4 million. But the general trend for fine 18th century furniture has been firmly downward in recent years and what was viewed as a rock solid investment category in the 1980's has fallen far from favour.

By contrast, 20th century furniture (along with 20th century art) has been leaping ahead. The Pop Art chair designed by Allen Jones in 1968 fetched £2.6 million. Carlo Mollino's oak and glass table (1949) was sold in New York in 2005 for $3.8 million. In 2015, the Lockheed Lounge designed by Marc Newson as recently as 1990 was sold for £2.5 million.

In the final analysis, all designers are at the mercy of capricious fashion. They may be unable to outrun the future but they can certainly shape the now.

Martin Waller

4

Erin Martin

Designer: Erin Martin. Company: Erin Martin Design, California, USA. Recent projects include a Spanish style home in Mill Valley, CA, Redd Wood restaurant in Yountville, CA and Eichler home in Palo Alto, CA. Current projects include Lucky Brand Flagship Store, in Manhattan Beach, CA, Four Seasons, Napa, CA and a mountain home in Park City, UT. Design philosophy: elegance is in the simplicity.

SCOTT   TRACY   JUDIJO   CAMERON

Kelly Hoppen

Designer: Kelly Hoppen. Company: Kelly Hoppen Interiors, London, UK. Specialising in luxury interior design in the UK and overseas including primary and secondary residences, yachts, planes, luxury resorts and boutique hotels. Recent work includes the Lux* Belle Mare resort in Mauritius, a bathware collection in collaboration with apaiser, a range of hotel fabrics for Richloom and a new collection of hotel furniture with Gervasoni. Design philosophy: a subtle coordinated fusion of East meets West, blended with warmth and opulence.

Kinney Chan

Designer: Kinney Chan. Company: Kinney Chan and Associates, Hong Kong. Specialising in interior design in Hong Kong, China and overseas including resorts and hotels, airport lounges, restaurants and bars, and luxury residential developments. Current projects include Plaza Premium airport lounges in Hong Kong, United Kingdom, Canada, China, India, Abu Dhabi, Maldives, Malaysia, Singapore & Macau, plus Café Bord de Mer, an award winning seaside hotel restaurant in Hong Kong and a show flat design for major property developers in mainland China. Design philosophy: creativity and originality are key.

Hare+Klein

Designer: Meryl Hare. Company: Hare + Klein, Sydney, Australia. Recent projects include an important listed property, a luxury motor yacht and a farmhouse in New South Wales. Current work includes major residences in Sydney, Melbourne and Adelaide. Design philosophy: to create original, creative interiors that stand the test of time & reflect the owners' lifestyle – as described in their recent book 'Colour Texture Comfort' published by Thames & Hudson.

 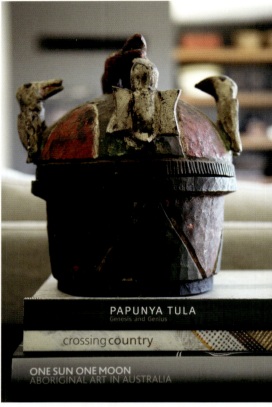

Chen Wu

Designer: Chen Wu. Company: New Metallurgical Group Design Consultants Ltd, Shenzhen, China. Specialising in commercial and entertainment spaces including clubhouses, restaurants, boutique hotels and brand design. Current projects include Wuxi Oscar bar, Xiamen Louis ONE and Agogo Red Star International KTV. Recent projects include Phoebe international, Taizhou, Kuala Lumpur, Malaysia. Design philosophy: stylish, rich, unique.

Stefano Dorata

Designer: Stefano Dorata. Company: Studio Dorata, Rome, Italy. Specialising in apartments, villas, yachts and hotels in Europe, America and Asia. Current projects include a villa in Florence, a seaside villa in Bali and a beach house in Porto Ercole. Recent work includes a loft in Rome, a hotel in Tel Aviv and an apartment in Milan along with the publication of his own book 'Houses by Stefano Dorata'. Design philosophy: simplicity and order.

Kit Kemp

Designer: Kit Kemp. Company: Firmdale Hotels, London, UK. A collection of nine hotels in London and New York designed by owner and design director, Kit Kemp in her award-winning luxurious, modern British style for which her innovative, exciting mix of colour, pattern, texture and art is world renowned. Current projects include Firmdale's second hotel in New York, The Whitby, set to open in 2016 and the tenth in the group. Recent work includes Ham Yard Hotel which opened in London's Soho in June 2014. Design philosophy: every piece of work is considered individual, with comfort, colour, wit and a certain carefree attitude.

Honky

Designer: Christopher Dezille. Company: Honky Architecture & Design, London, UK. An award winning practice offering a luxury comprehensive design service to private clients, property developers and boutique hotels in the UK and overseas. Current work includes a number of projects for developers, a substantial property in Marbella and a triplex penthouse in Southwark. Recent projects include an apartment in Cannes, a family home in Wimbledon, a property in Richmond and several apartments across London. Design philosophy: innovation, quality and service.

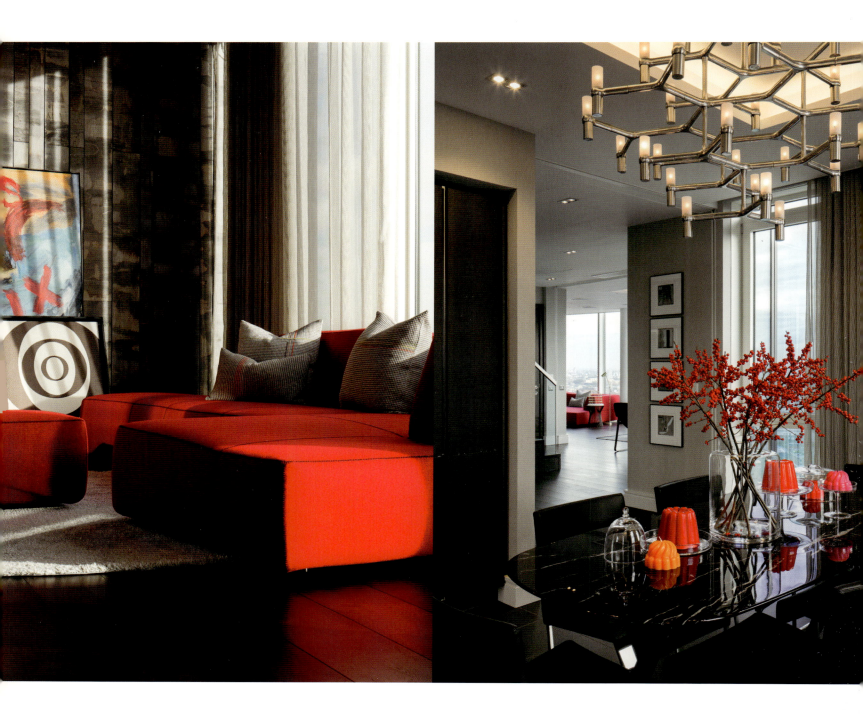

Aleksandra Laska

Designer: Aleksandra Laska. Company: Ola Laska, Warsaw, Poland. Specialising in creating timeless interiors. Recent projects include the partial remodeling of the National Opera House, a 1,700 sq m showroom in Warsaw and an artist's studio. Current work includes a 230 sq m historic apartment in Warsaw, an antique shop and a 16th century house both in Krakow. Design philosophy: commitment, complication, harmony.

Katya Fedorchenko

Designer: Katya Fedorchenko. Company: Katya Fedorchenko Architectural Bureau, Moscow, Russia. Specialising in private and commercial work in Moscow. Recent projects include a 600 sq m, 360° view penthouse with a roof terrace in the centre of Moscow, a 3,000 sq m contemporary style residence with guest houses near Moscow as well as a hunting mansion. Current work includes a house and several apartments in the centre of Moscow. Design philosophy: artistic, joyful, different.

Elevation Partners

Designers: Arcturus Lau, Alex Yim, Wilson To, Ivan Wong. Company: Elevation Partners Co. Ltd, Hong Kong. Specialising in clubhouses, show suites, luxury residential developments, sales offices, restaurants and offices. Current projects include a luxury residential development clubhouse in Sai Kung, Hong Kong, a residential complex in Taipa, Macau and a riverside development in Foshan. Recent work includes a sales office and show suite in Guangzhou, a residential complex in a new development district, Hong Kong and an exclusive suite in Hong Kong. Design philosophy: every space is special; every solution is unique.

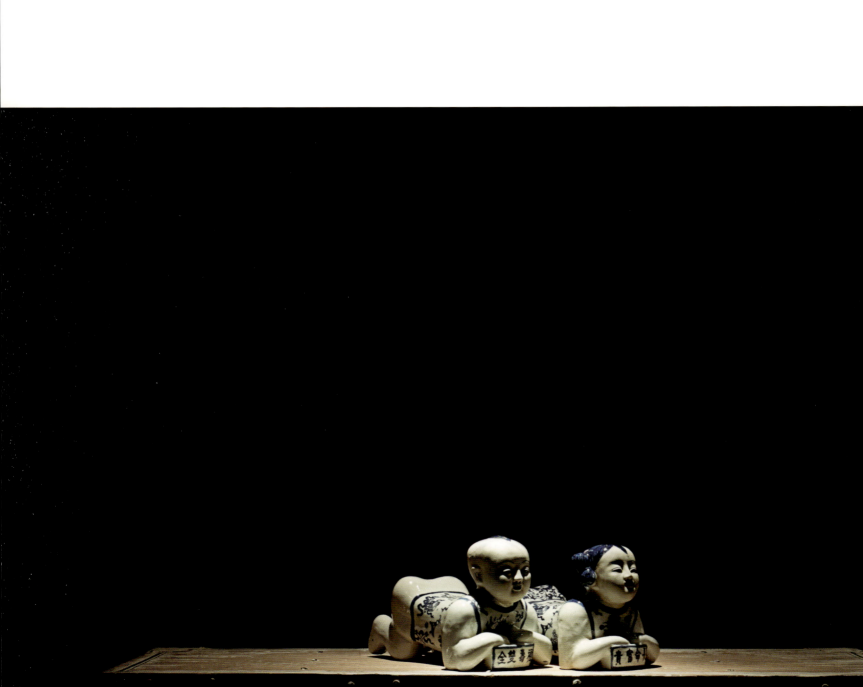

Jeffreys Interiors

Designer: Alison Vance. Company: Jeffreys Interiors, Edinburgh, Scotland. Recent projects include two city centre townhouses converted into the global headquarters of a digital media company with off the wall design including client cocktail bar and graffiti clad inspiration room. Current work includes a private club in Yorkshire, a yacht in Italy and a castle in the highlands. Design philosophy: to bring quality and comfort to each project, challenging concepts of both contemporary and traditional.

Collection Privée

Designers: Nicolette Schouten & Marianne Pellerin. Company: Collection Privée, Cannes, France. Specialising in some of the world's most beautiful properties. Recent work includes a penthouse in Cannes, a large contemporary house in Villefranche-sur-Mer and an 18th century castle in Fayence. Current projects include a beach front house and beach club restaurant in Saint-Tropez and an apartment in Gstaad. Design philosophy: original, eclectic and refined.

Sherry Hayslip

Designer: Sherry Hayslip. Company: Hayslip Design Associates, Texas, USA. Specialising in luxury interior design in America and overseas, including both primary and secondary homes, hotel apartments and boutique office spaces. Current projects include a ranch in Los Valles, Texas, an estate in the Sonoma wine country and a multi-purpose entertainment pavilion for collectable cars and art installations. Recent work includes a reinterpretation of Chanel's Parisian apartment at the International Art, Antique and Jewellery show, a substantial beach home in Flower Hill, Jamaica and various major residential homes in Dallas, Texas. Design philosophy: devoted to client satisfaction.

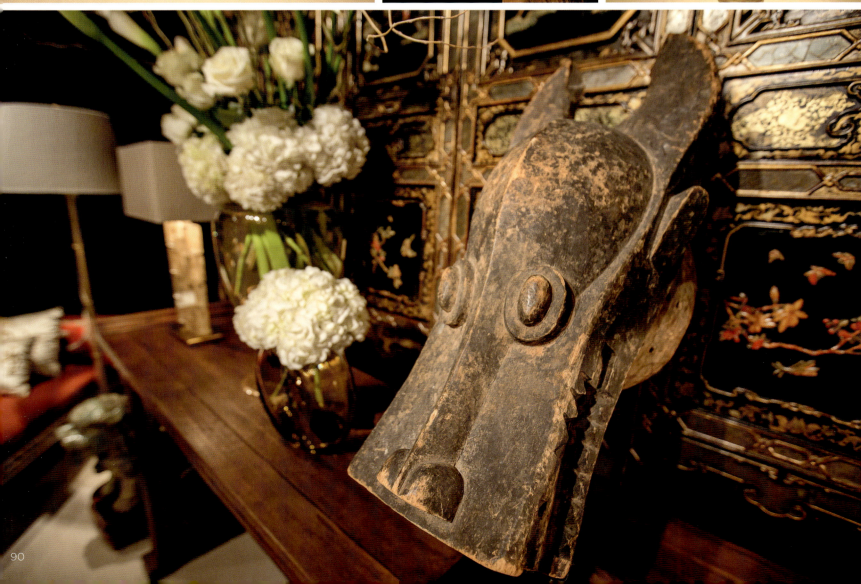

Katharine Pooley

Designer: Katharine Pooley. Company: Katharine Pooley Ltd, Knightsbridge, London. Katharine and her team create some of the most desirable homes in the world. Recent work includes an apartment in Lancaster Gate, London, a St Regis lateral apartment, Singapore and the entire redesign of a 10,000 sq ft residence in Grosvenor Square, Mayfair. Current projects include a 5,000 sq ft villa in Cap-Martin, South of France, a 15,000 sq ft Belgravia town house, London and an apartment in central Paris. Design philosophy: imaginative design, exquisitely realised.

Holger Kaus

Designer: Holger Kaus, Miesbach, Germany. Specialising in luxury interior architecture and landscape design internationally, including residential developments, chalets and mountain resorts, country houses and homes throughout Europe. Recent projects include an estate in Ibiza and in N E Spain, plus apartments in Berlin, Frankfurt and Munich. Current projects include private houses near Frankfurt and the Austrian countryside. Design philosophy: to fulfil their client's wishes, tailoring eclectic, comfortable design, respectful of art and antiques.

PTang Studio

Designers: Philip Tang & Brian Ip. Company: PTang Studio Ltd., Hong Kong. Specialising in luxury interior architecture in Hong Kong and overseas including both primary and secondary private homes, residential developments and show flats. Current projects include a residential development with sales gallery and a number of show flats in Cebu, Philippines, a series of show flats in The Grace, Hong Kong and The Langham Hotel in Haining, China. Design philosophy: focus on basics, create comfort and atmosphere.

SAARANHA&
VASCONCELOS

Designers: Carmo Aranha & Rosario Tello. Company: SA&V – SAARANHA&VASCONCELOS, Lisbon, Portugal. A predominantly residential portfolio, with some commercial work including private yachts. Recent projects include a rural property complex in Alentejo, a chalet in Switzerland and a villa in Boston. Current work includes villas in Vale do Lobo, Algarve, Cascais and Chengdu, China. Design philosophy: connection, commitment, contrast, coherence.

NEM TUDO É VERDADE

THE
SHOW
MUST
GO
HOME

Gloria Cortina

Designer: Gloria Cortina. Company: Gloria Cortina Estudio, Lomas Virreyes, Mexico. Specialising in high end interior design in Mexico and overseas, including both primary and secondary private homes, luxury residential developments and boutique hotels. Current projects include Reforma penthouse in Mexico City, a Beach Club in Cabo San Lucas and an equestrian ranch in Valle de Bravo Mexico. Design philosophy: clean, contemporary, bespoke.

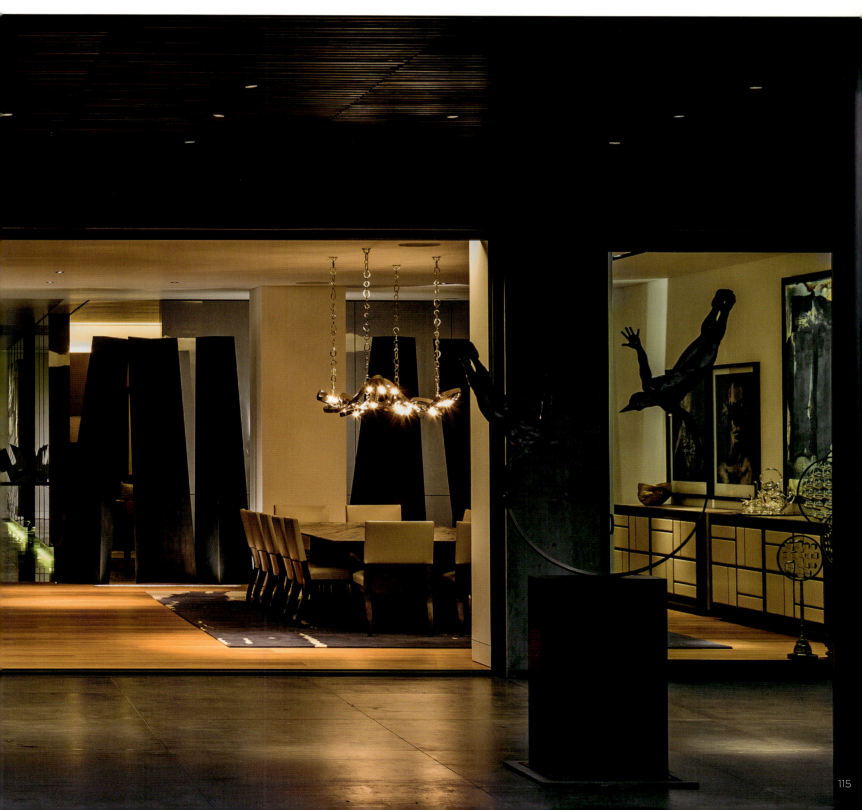

Lígia Casanova

Designer: Lígia Casanova. Company: Atelier Lígia Casanova, Lisbon, Portugal. Specialising in both public and residential spaces in Portugal and overseas. Current projects include a set of apartments for luxury rental in Lisbon, a villa in the centre of Portugal and a penthouse in São Paulo. Recent work includes apartments in Lisbon, Porto and Algarve, a beach house in Comporta and Quinta do Lago. Design philosophy: to make room for happiness.

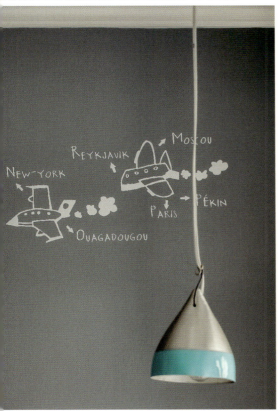

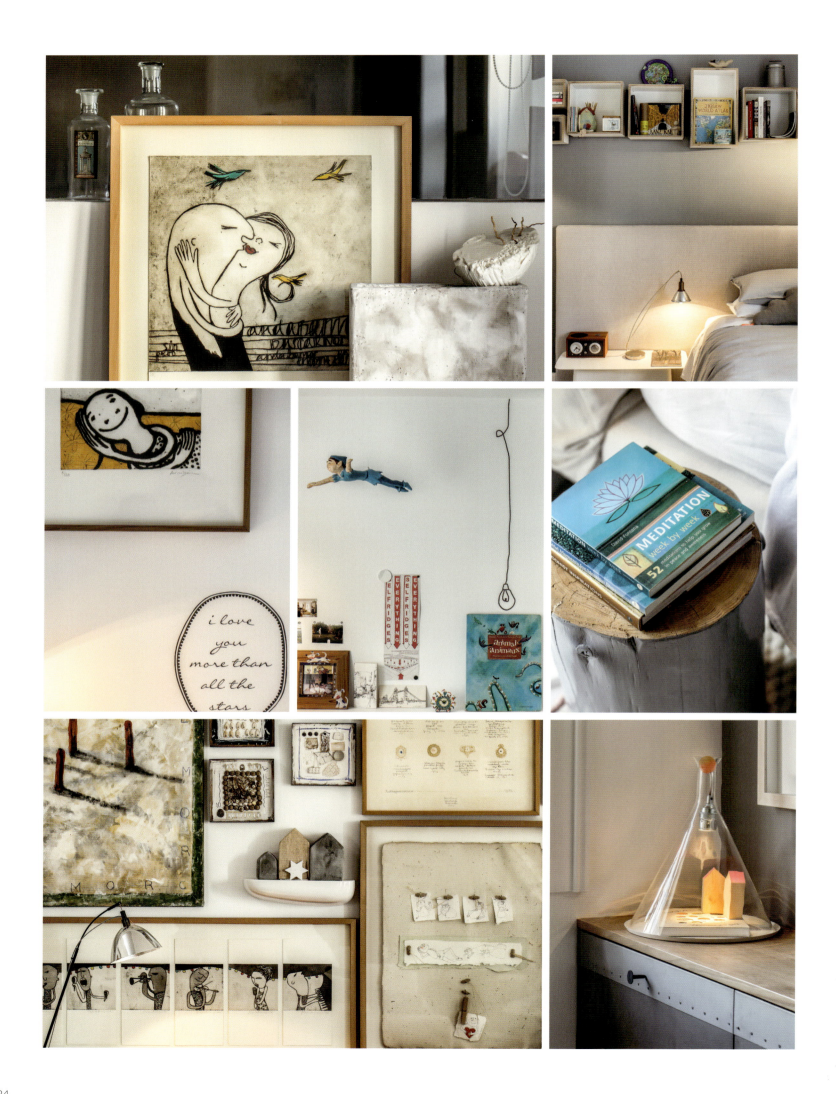

Rooshad Shroff

Designer: Rooshad Shroff. Company: Rooshad Shroff Architecture + Design, Mumbai, India. A multi disciplinary design firm, specialising in a variety of architecture, interiors, furniture and product design within India and overseas. Recent projects include a 3,000 sq ft private villa in Kodaikanal, Southern India, a 15,000 sq ft residential interior in Mumbai for a heritage bungalow and a 1,200 sq ft ski lodge in Daisen, Japan. Recent work includes a 1,000 sq ft Christian Louboutin boutique in Bangkok, a 2,500 sq ft part retail, part restaurant in Jaipur and a 1,200 sq ft show apartment in Mumbai for Oberoi Realty. Design philosophy: custom made design which celebrates the crafts of the Indian artisan.

One Plus

Designers: Ajax Law Ling Kit and Virginia Lung Wai Ki. Company: One Plus Partnership, Hong Kong. In 2012, One Plus became the first Asian overall winner of the Andrew Martin Interior Designer of the Year. Current work includes several major cinema projects and an exclusive clubhouse in China. Recent projects include a cinema in Causeway Bay and sales offices in Hong Kong and China. Design philosophy: bold and divergent.

Debra Cronin

Designer: Debra Cronin. Company: Debra Cronin Design, Sydney, Australia. Specialising in high end residential and boutique commercial projects. Current work includes a heritage listed sandstone family home in Balmain, a penthouse apartment overlooking Bondi Beach and a log cabin on the Hawksbury River. Recent projects include a substantial terraced house in Woollahra and a block of Art Déco apartments in Potts Point. Design philosophy: Alice in Wonderland meets the Adams family. As unique as a snowflake, only cooler.

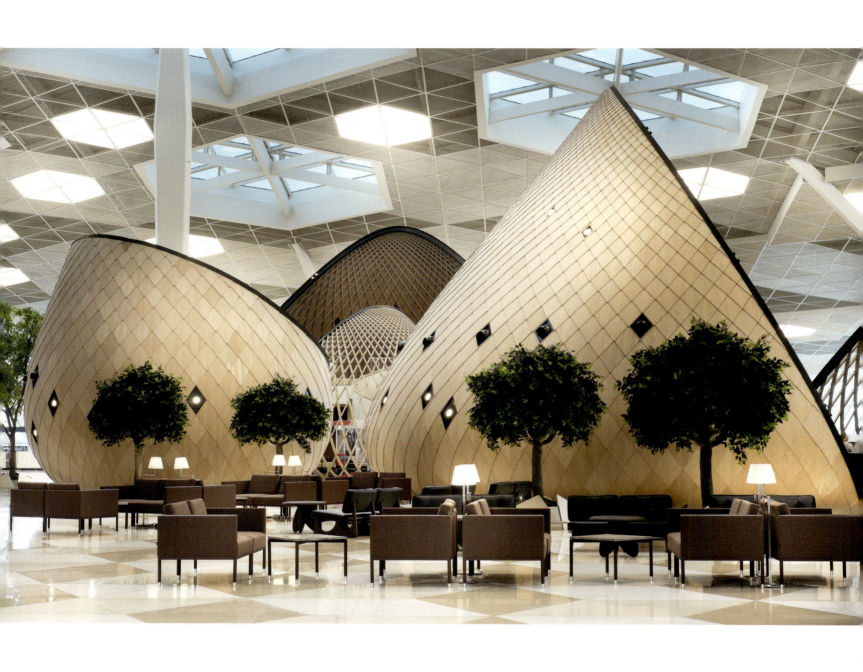

Autoban

Designers: Seyhan Özdemir & Sefer Çağlar. Company: Autoban, Istanbul, Turkey. An internationally renowned, multidisciplinary design studio. Recent projects include Babaji Turkish restaurant in London, Duck and Rice Chinese restaurant in London and 45,000 sq m of interior relaxation space at Bakü Heydar Aliyev Airport. Current work includes three buildings at NEF Sütlüce residence complex in the historic area of Istanbul, a 45 m private yacht and the renovation of one of the world's largest hotel chains in Istanbul. Design philosophy: challenge convention, celebrate form and enhance function.

LSD CASA

Designer: Kot Ge. Company: LSD CASA, Shenzhen, China. With branches and offices in Hong Kong, Beijing and further afield, LSD CASA specialise in domestic and private work, commercial and office spaces, clubs, villas and show flats. Recent projects include Vanke Junxi Villa in Hangzhou, Vanke Emerald Riverside House in Shanghai and Vanke Firenze Villa in Shanghai. Current work includes One&Only Sanya Resort Hotel in Hainan, V7 North Lake Heights Private Club in Beijing and High Fenghua of Greenland Sales Pavilion & Gallery and showrooms in Shanghai. Design philosophy: beyond trends.

Designer: Marina Filippova. Company: Marina Filippova Designs, Moscow, Russia. Commissions include residential, hospitality, retail and office spaces in the UK, Italy and Russia. Current projects include a villa in Italy, a spa in the UK and a club house in Moscow. Recent work includes a restaurant and wellness centre, an office in Moscow, and apartments in London, Moscow and St. Petersburg. Design philosophy: timeless interiors for everyday enjoyment.

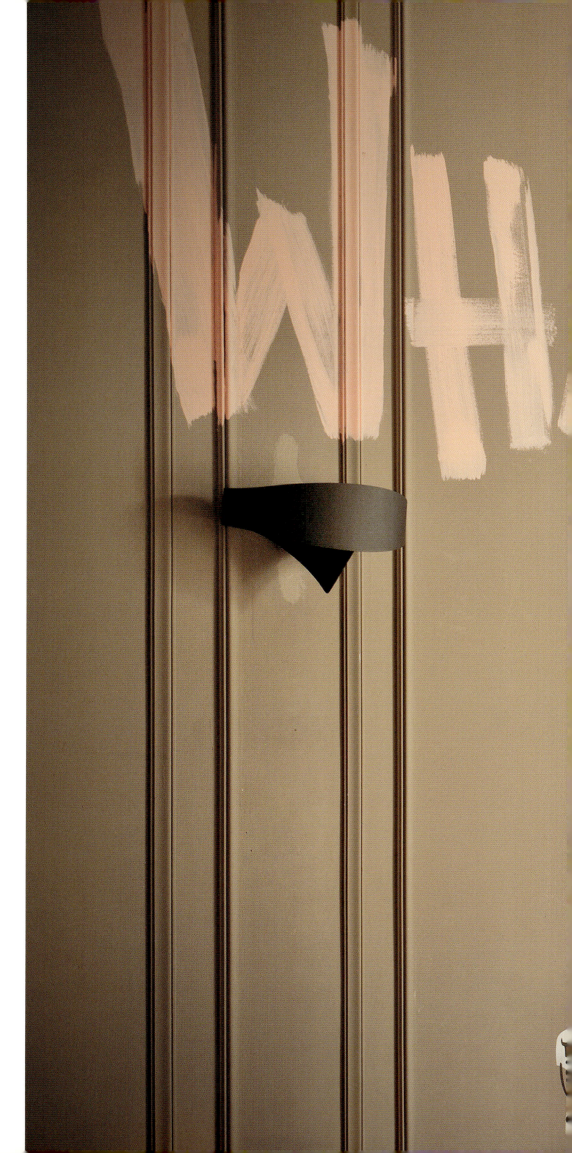

Marina Filippova

Sorry!
The lifestyle you
ordered is currently
out of stock

Fiona Barratt-Campbell

Designer: Fiona Barratt-Campbell. Company: Fiona Barratt Interiors, London, UK. Luxury residential and commercial projects in the UK and overseas. Current work includes an exclusive apartment in Moscow, a four storey townhouse in Mayfair and a large family house in Yorkshire. Recent projects include a beach house in Mallorca, a private residence in Knightsbridge and a development of three luxury apartments in Hyde Park. Design philosophy: fluid and elegant.

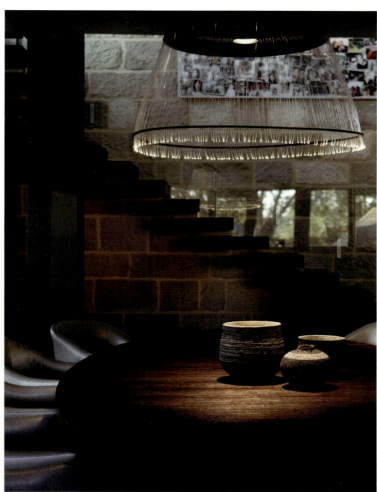

Sarah Davison

Designer: Sarah Davison. Company: Sarah Davison Interior Design, Paddington, Australia. Known for highly considered, beautifully planned residential design. Current projects include a cliff front house overlooking Manly Beach NSW, a barrister's chambers in the new Deutsche Bank building, Sydney and a penthouse apartment with beautiful views of Double Bay, NSW. Recent work includes a penthouse apartment in Kuala Lumpur, a large family home on Palm Beach, north of Sydney and a pavilion style home in Mittagong in the NSW Southern Highlands. Design philosophy: function, quality, beauty.

Suna

Designers: Rebecca Tucker & Helen Fewster. Suna Interior Design, London, UK. An award winning interior design consultancy providing services for property developers and the hospitality industry. Current projects include a development in South West London, a family home in Cambridge and a contemporary apartment in East London. Recent work includes a townhouse on Portobello, a luxury property in Hove and a house in Hampshire. Design philosophy: tailor made and bespoke.

Sophie Ashby

Designer: Sophie Ashby. Company: Studio Ashby Ltd, London, UK. Specialising in residential interior design and luxury residential developments and restaurants. Current projects include a villa in the South of France, a penthouse apartment in the South Bank Tower in London and a family townhouse in Chelsea. Recent work includes an apartment in King's Cross, a seaside house in Devon and a home in Covent Garden. Design philosophy: authentic, eclectic, unique.

Chou Yi

Designer: Chou Yi. Company: Joy Interior Design Studio, Taichung, Taiwan. Specialising in public areas and private residences as well as commercial projects. Current work includes a hotpot restaurant in Kaohsiung City and a hotel and pasta restaurant in Taichung. Recent projects include a barbecue restaurant in Taichung, a hotpot restaurant in Taipei and an aquatic restaurant in Taichung. Design philosophy: the poetry of space, the feeling of people, the precision of detail.

Designer: Nicola Koster. Company: Nicola Koster Interiors, Stellenbosch, South Africa. Specialising in domestic interiors for both primary and secondary homes. Recent projects include a home on a golfing estate, Hermanus, SA and a house in Stellenbosch and Constatia, Cape Town. Current work includes a farmhouse in Paarl, Western Cape and two further homes in Constantia. Design philosophy: blend antiques with modern to add character and edge.

Nicola Koster

Allison Paladino

Designer: Allison Paladino. Company: Allison Paladino Interior Design and Collections, Florida, USA. Specialising in ocean side estates in Palm Beach and summer residences in New York as well as product design, lighting, furniture, rug and art collections. Current projects include a Palm Beach seaside retreat and estate and a thoroughbred horse farm in Ocala, Florida. Recent work includes a home in Rye, New York on Long Island Sound. Design philosophy: sophisticated, welcoming, comfortable design to suit our clients' vision.

Zeynep Fadillioglu

Designer: Zeynep Fadillioglu. Company: Zeynep Fadillioglu Design, Istanbul, Turkey. Specialising in luxury interior architecture in Europe, the Middle East and overseas. Current projects include luxurious mansions in Oman, India and Jordan, a seaside restaurant & club in Southern Turkey, boutiques in Munich and London as well as major residential homes and executive offices in Istanbul. Recent work includes a shop in Geneva, a grand residential building in Istanbul, beach houses in Southern Turkey and a Bosphorus mansion in Istanbul. Design philosophy: fusing Eastern and Western aesthetics for universal appeal.

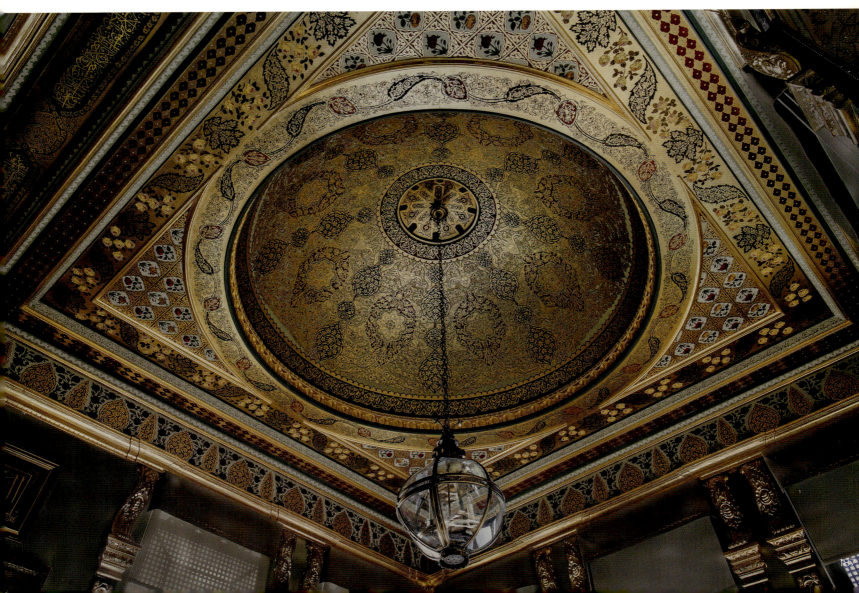

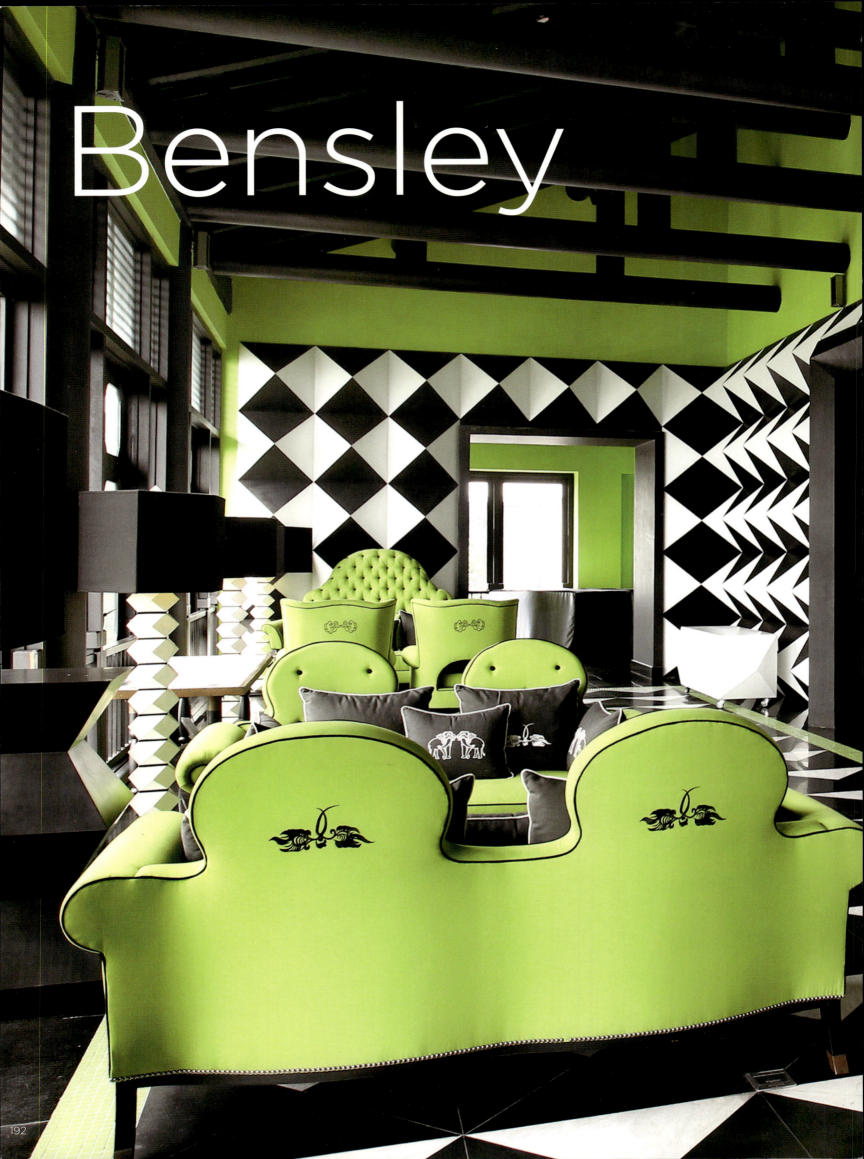

Bensley

Designer: Bill Bensley. Company: BENSLEY, Bangkok & Bali. Providing unique solutions for resorts, hotels, private homes and palaces. Current projects include The Waldorf Astoria in Ubud, Bali, The Four Seasons in LiJiang, China and The Ritz Rerve, Phu Quoc, Vietnam. Recent work includes The Siam, a boutique hotel in Bangkok, The Four Seasons at the Golden Triangle, Chiang Rai, Thailand and the new flagship property for the Intercontinental, Danang. Design philosophy: the odder the better.

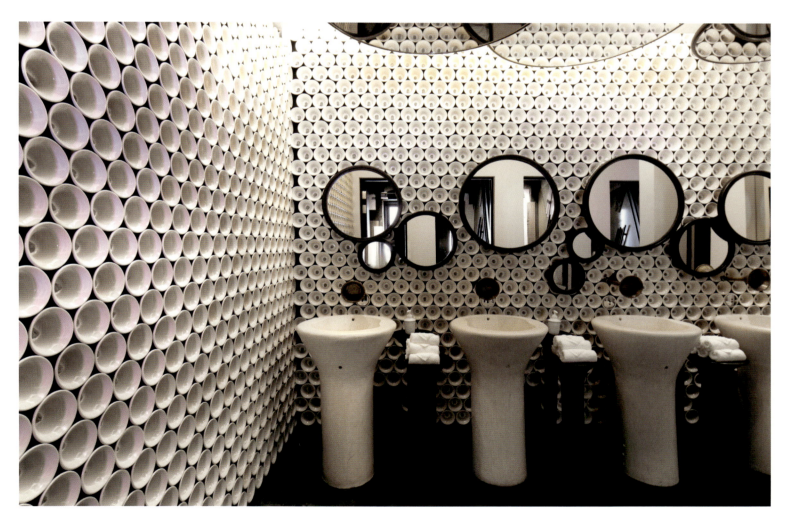

White & Kaki

Designers: Carlos Rocha & Vitor Duarte. Company: White & Kaki, Algarve, Portugal. Specialising in luxury interior design in Portugal and all over Europe. Recent work includes a showroom in Lisbon, an office in Vilamoura and two houses in Quinta do Lago. Current projects include a house in Vilamoura and a house in Dunas Douradas. Design philosophy: decoration with the world inside.

Casa do
Passadiço

Designers: Catarina Rosas, Cláudia and Catarina Soares Pereira. Company: Casa do Passadiço, Braga, Portugal. An award winning team, specialising in private residences, yachts and commercial spaces. Current projects include the recently opened shoe label Aquazzura flagship store in historic Palazzo Corsini, Florence as well as the headquarters and offices for the brand. The team have also recently delivered luxurious residences in Lisbon, Quinta do Lago, Algarve, Estoril and Luanda, Angola. Design philosophy: contemporary elegance with discreet luxury.

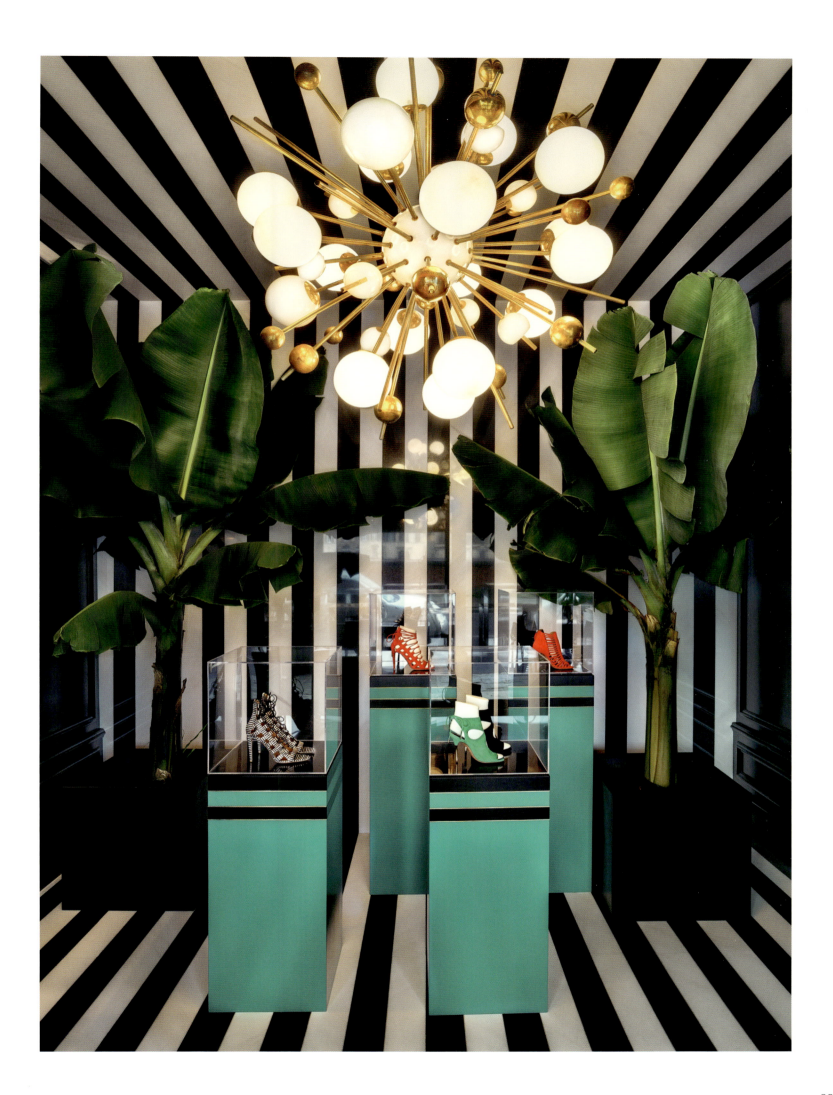

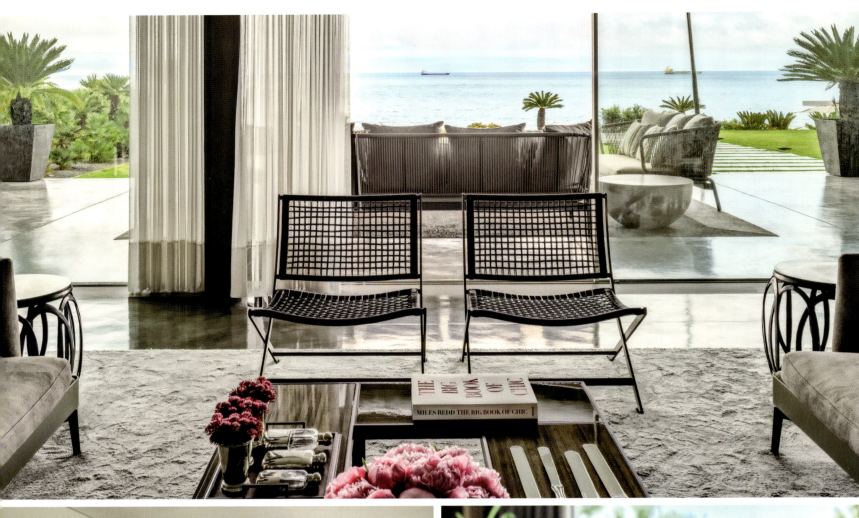

Jay Jeffers

Designer: Jay Jeffers. Company: Jeffers Design Group, California, USA. Specialising in interior architecture and design for luxury private homes, developments and boutique hotels. Recent work includes a 2-level apartment on 5th Avenue in New York, the Ritz-Carlton Private Residences, Lake Tahoe and an estate in Woodside, California. Current projects include a vacation home in Lake Tahoe, an historic estate and family barn in the Napa Valley and a home in the Pacific Heights neighbourhood of San Francisco. Design philosophy: chic, curated, livable, sprinkled with whimsy.

THE LOVE METER

HIS

To-Nites the Nite — of course

Just ask me? — SURE — Say Please

Any-time — ok. — READY

HERS

I've got a headache! — I'm awful tired! — I'm not speaking!

TONITES THE NITE! — COAX

I'm sleepy!

Alexandra Schauer

Designer: Alexandra Schauer. Company: ALISCHA Interior Design, Vienna, Austria. Specialising in luxury interior design, planning and project management for high end projects in Austria, Germany, Spain and Russia including drafts and plans for new residences as well as the revitalisation of existing properties. Current work includes a palace in Vienna, a majestic estate overlooking the sea in Ibiza and the renovation of a private chalet in Kitzbühel. Recent projects include an exclusive apartment in Moscow, a super yacht in Spain and a unique mansion in Salzburg. Design philosophy: modern and classic.

Sherwood Design

Designer: Shuheng Huang. Company: Sherwood Design Inc. Taipei, Taiwan. Specialising in project planning, architectural design, interior planning, landscape design and furniture development. Recent work includes a luxury house in Guizhou Province and clubhouses in the new area of Taipei City. Current projects include a show flat in Shenzhen and a clubhouse and villa in the Taipei mountains. Design philosophy: balance classical with modern, East with West, artificial with natural.

Kathleen Hay

Designer: Kathleen Hay. Company: Kathleen Hay Designs, Nantucket, USA. Specialising in high end new builds for the luxury home market, including primary and secondary residences, summer houses, and boutique commercial projects. Recent work includes a converted factory mill into a duplex apartment in Brooklyn, a state of the art, LEED certified Music School and a penthouse apartment in Boston. Current projects include a large farmhouse in New Canaan, Connecticut, several beach houses and guest cottages on Nantucket Island and the renovation of a barn into a guest house in upper New York. Design philosophy: clean lined and simply appointed interiors that evoke sophistication and elegance without sacrificing comfort and functionality. Rooms that whisper 'come live in me.'

Karen Howes

Designer: Karen Howes. Company: Taylor Howes Designs, London, UK. Award winning International design practice, offering a comprehensive, luxury design service to private clients, property developers and hoteliers. Current projects include a residential villa in Abu Dhabi, a large new build in Surrey and a private apartment in Kensington. Recent work includes a marketing suite and two show apartments for a developer in Kensington, a 9-storey townhouse in Kensington and a private apartment in Knightsbridge. Design philosophy: creative excellence, caring service.

George Efthimiou

www.tinos-ehouses.gr

Designer: George Efthimiou. Company: G. Efthimiou Ltd, Athens, Greece. Specialising in luxury interior design for offices, residential developments, hotels and private yachts in Greece, Monaco, Switzerland, New York and London. Current projects include apartments in Geneva and Athens plus a Michelin star restaurant also in Athens. Recent work includes a house on a Greek island, a loft in New York and an apartment in Beirut. Design philosophy: dreams into reality.

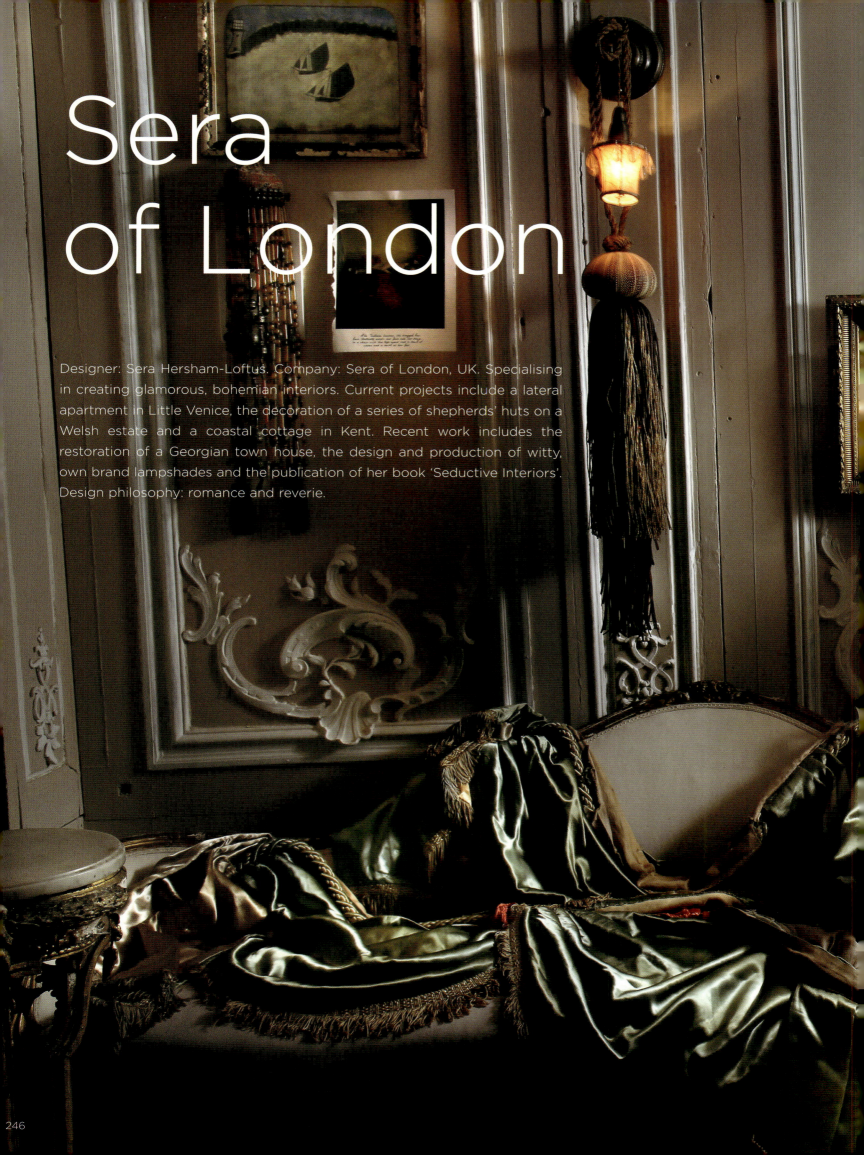

Sera
of London

Designer: Sera Hersham-Loftus. Company: Sera of London, UK. Specialising in creating glamorous, bohemian interiors. Current projects include a lateral apartment in Little Venice, the decoration of a series of shepherds' huts on a Welsh estate and a coastal cottage in Kent. Recent work includes the restoration of a Georgian town house, the design and production of witty, own brand lampshades and the publication of her book 'Seductive Interiors'. Design philosophy: romance and reverie.

Joanna Wood

Designer: Joanna Wood. Company: Joanna Trading Ltd, London, UK. Recognised as one of Britain's leading figures in the international world of interior design. Current projects include a Chinese Chippendale ballroom, the restoration of a 1720's manor house in Gloucestershire and a bachelor pad in Belgravia. Recent work includes a large private chalet in Gstaad, a penthouse in Central London and the restructuring of The All England Lawn Tennis Club. Design philosophy: comfortable, elegant and tailored design with a contemporary and eclectic approach.

Janine Lazard

Designers: Janine Lazard and Jessica Harrisberg. Company: Janine Lazard Interiors, Cape Town & Johannesburg, South Africa. Specialising in luxury residential interior design in South Africa and abroad. Current work includes a large family home in Clifton CT, an apartment in Regent's Park, London and a high rise apartment in the Michelangelo Towers in Sandton, Johannesburg. Recent projects include a beach side bungalow in Cape Town, an apartment in the V&A waterfront in Cape Town and small boutique offices in Sandton, Johannesburg. Design philosophy: contemporary, classic, clean.

Krista Hartmann

Designer: Krista Hartmann. Company: Krista Hartmann Interiør AS, Oslo, Norway. Predominantly large residential projects with some commercial work in and around Norway. Current work includes a contemporary summer house by the coast in South Norway, a large penthouse flat with fabulous views and a new wedding shop in Oslo. Recent projects include a hunting lodge in the forest, a new fusion restaurant in Oslo and a spectacular office for a shipping company. Design philosophy: make dreams come true.

Alexandra Kidd

Designer: Alexandra Kidd. Company: Alexandra Kidd Design, Sydney, Australia. Specialising in a broad range of residential and commercial interiors. Recent work includes the complete renovation of a three story home overlooking Sydney Harbour, the design of a nurturing space for Sydney's Mater Hospital Neo-Natal Special Care Nursery and the redesign of an original P&O style home on Sydney's Eastern beaches. Current projects include furnishing a Sydney family home in collaboration with an award-winning international architect, a development for a holiday home in the South of France and reimagining the interiors for an existing waterfront dwelling in Sydney. Design philosophy: the belief that well considered design can change lives.

Designer: Douglas Mackie. Company: D Mackie Design, London, UK. Specialising in residential interiors in London and worldwide. Recent work includes a large scale project in the Middle East, a house in Provence and a 4 year renovation of an important house in Chelsea. Current projects include further work in the Middle East, a Tudor house in London and a house in Belgravia. Design philosophy: layered, considered, tailored, sophisticated.

Douglas Mackie

Designer: Rosa May Sampaio. Company: Rosa May Decoração de Interiores, São Paulo, Brazil. Recent ongoing projects include a 700 sq m office in São Paulo, a 1,000 sq m country house in São Paulo and a 500 sq m oceanfront apartment in Ipanema, Rio de Janeiro. Other work includes La Barra Golf Club in Punta del Este, Estancia America, a 3,000 sq m farm in Argentina and the residential compounds of the Marquee of Salamanca in Santa Teresa, Rio de Janeiro. Design philosophy: harmony and well being.

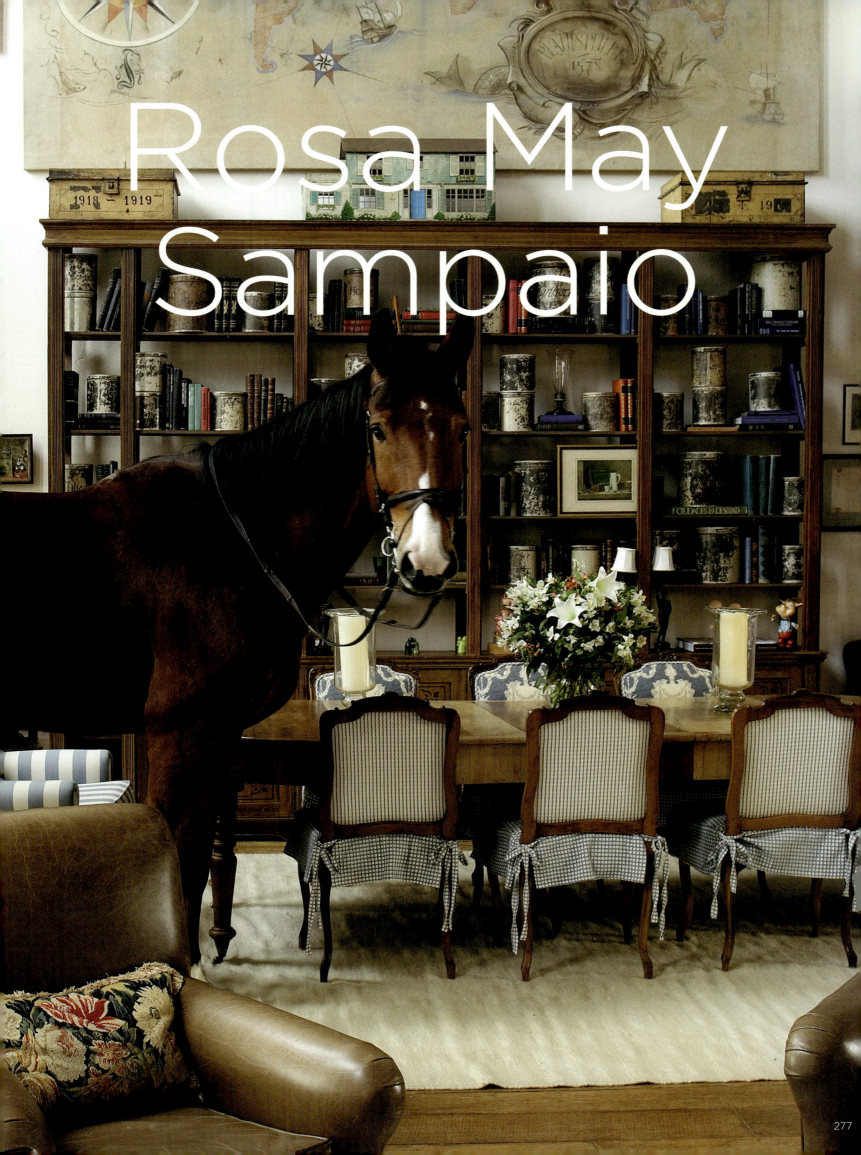

Rosa May Sampaio

Ryu Kosaka

Designer: Ryu Kosaka. Company: A.N.D. NOMURA Co; Ltd, Tokyo, Japan. Specialising in high end commercial space design. Current projects include a restaurant and a clinic in Tokyo, a sushi restaurant in Singapore and a retail store in Hong Kong. Recent work includes a Changchun Villa and a Japanese restaurant in Fukuoka. Design philosophy: more than immaculate spaces to embrace relationship, sensitivity and emotion.

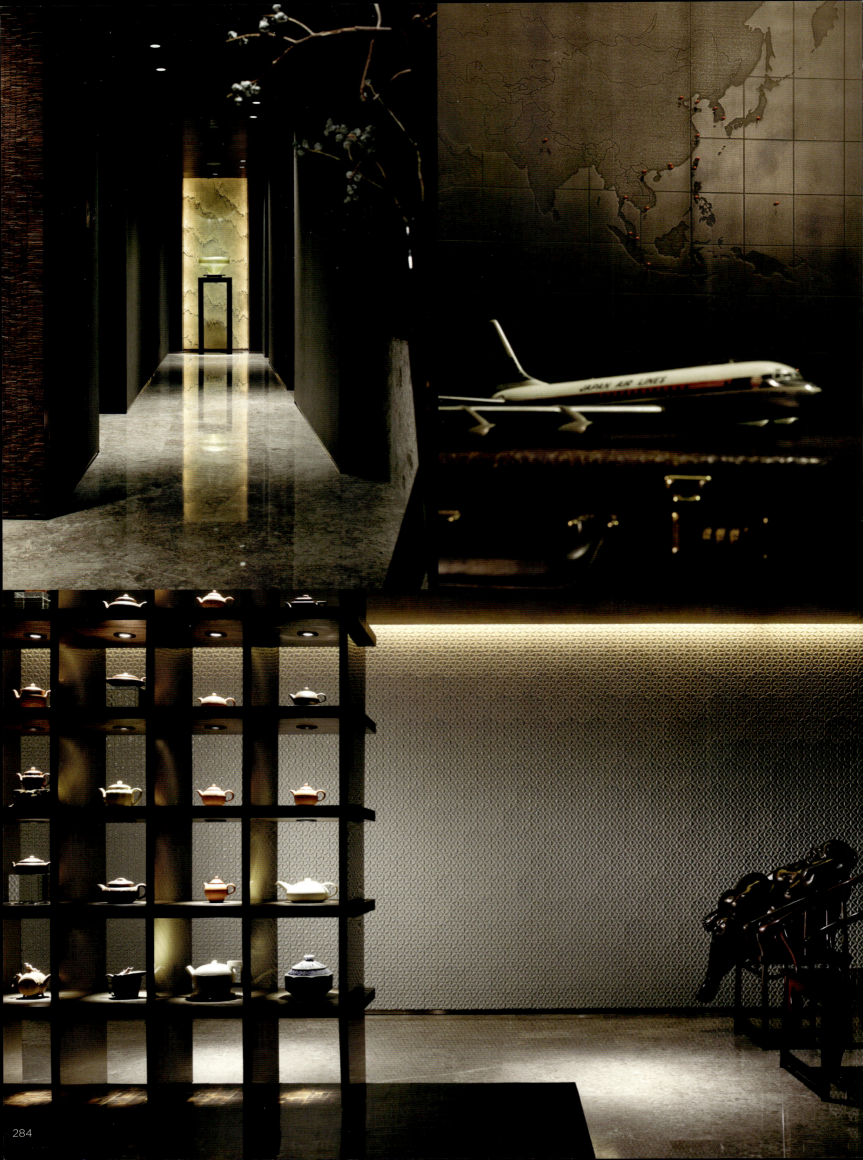

Les Ensembliers

Designers: Richard Ouellette and Maxime Vandal. Company: Les Ensembliers, Montreal, Canada. Predominantly private, high end residences and estates in North America and overseas. Current projects include an historic 4,000 sq ft apartment in Paris, a 7,000 sq ft penthouse in Montreal and exclusive seaside villas in Palm Beach. Recent work includes remodeling a 6,000 sq ft multilevel penthouse in an old converted sugar mill in Montreal, a significant renovation of a house in Palm Beach and a private hunting estate in Northern Quebec. Design philosophy: building meaning into beauty.

Heidi Meyer

Designer: Heidi Meyer. Company: Yohm, Queensland, Australia. Specialising in residential and commercial spaces worldwide. Recent projects include a luxurious waterfront apartment in Mooloolaba, Queensland, the renovation of an 11th century medieval watchtower overlooking Mont Blanc and the restoration of a 1920's bungalow in Auckland. Current projects include a six star eco lodge on the Sunshine Coast of Australia, a minimalist apartment in Primrose Hill, London and an overwater bungalow in Bora Bora. Design philosophy: to marry the bold, with the understated, to create fun and playful spaces that provoke the ultimate sensory experience.

TDC & Associates

Designer: LH Chan. Company: TDC & Associates Pte Ltd, Singapore. A leading firm specialising in luxurious, high end private residences and development projects in Singapore, Malaysia & Indonesia. Current work includes a holiday home in Southern Malaysia, a duplex penthouse in Singapore and a bungalow at Braddell Hill in Singapore. Recent projects include a duplex apartment in Scotts Road, Singapore, a bungalow in Jakarta and another beside the MacRitchie reservoir forest reserve in Singapore. Design philosophy: to create quality, lasting and functional projects.

ARRCC

Designers: Mark Rielly, Jon Case & Michele Rhoda. Company: ARRCC, Cape Town, South Africa. Work is international, including domestic, hospitality, corporate, retail and leisure sectors. Recent projects include the refurbishment of the historic Alphen Hotel in Constantia, Cape Town, a luxurious villa at the resort of Eden Island in the Seychelles and a penthouse apartment in Passeig de Gràcia, Barcelona. Current work includes a private villa on Star Island, Miami, a luxury villa development in Shenzhen and a villa resort development in Bodrum, Turkey. Design philosophy: luxurious, seductive, understated.

Chang Ching-Ping

Designer: Chang Ching-Ping. Company: Tienfun Interior Planning Co Ltd, Taichung, Taiwan. Specialising in luxury interior architecture in China and overseas including private homes, residential developments and boutique hotels. Current projects include a private club in Shenzhen, a hotel in Taitung and a lobby in Taichung. Design philosophy: integrated, dynamic, meticulous.

Pamela
Makin

Designer: Pamela Makin. Company: Les Interieurs, Sydney, Australia. A boutique design practice known for creating unique interiors. Recent projects include the restoration of a heritage terrace house in Sydney, a family estate in Balmoral, apartments in Kings Cross and a beach house overlooking the Pacific Ocean. Design philosophy: Pamela channels Orson Welles 'create your own visual style, let it be unique for yourself, yet identifiable to others.'

Kris Lin

Designer: Kris Lin. Company: KLID (Kris Lin Interior Design). Projects are international and currently include a sales office in Shanghai, a tea house in Changzou and a club in Guangzhou. Recent work includes two sales offices in Ningbo and Shanghai, a club in Xiamen as well as apartments in Hampstead, Regent's Park and Kensington, a beach house in Barbados and a large family home in Wimbledon. Design philosophy: to look at the world with open and generous eyes.

Francisco Neves

Designer: Francisco Neves. Company: 5 Janelas Interior Design, Guimarães, Portugal. Specialising in private and commercial work. Recent projects include a beach house in the Algarve, an art gallery and apartments in the city. Ongoing work includes two hotel suites, a restaurant and a bar. Design philosophy: inspired by travel, cinema and books.

Angelos Angelopoulos

Designer: Angelos Angelopoulos. Company: Angelos Angelopoulos, Athens, Greece. Specialising in a range of developments in Greece and overseas. Recent projects include a chalet in Greece, two residences in Athens and the planning of a residence in Florida. Current work includes a large scale resort hotel in Cyprus, a boutique hotel and the design of a food chain, both in Athens. Design philosophy: understand psychology, cure through aesthetics.

Flora Lau

Designer: Flora Lau. Company: Flora Lau Designers Limited, Hong Kong. Specialising in luxury interior design in China. Current projects include a villa in Shenzhen, a sales centre and club house in Hangzhou and a show flat in Shenzhen. Recent work includes loft apartments, a commercial office and a sales centre in Nanjing. Design philosophy: enjoyment and participation.

Nastya Komarova

Designer: Nastya Komarova. Company: Nastya Komarova Design, Moscow, Russia. Specialising in luxury private and public interiors in Russia as well as worldwide. Current projects include three country houses near Moscow, a seaside apartment in Nice and another in Prague. Design philosophy: to create harmonious homes that make the owners always feel happy to come back to.

João Mansur

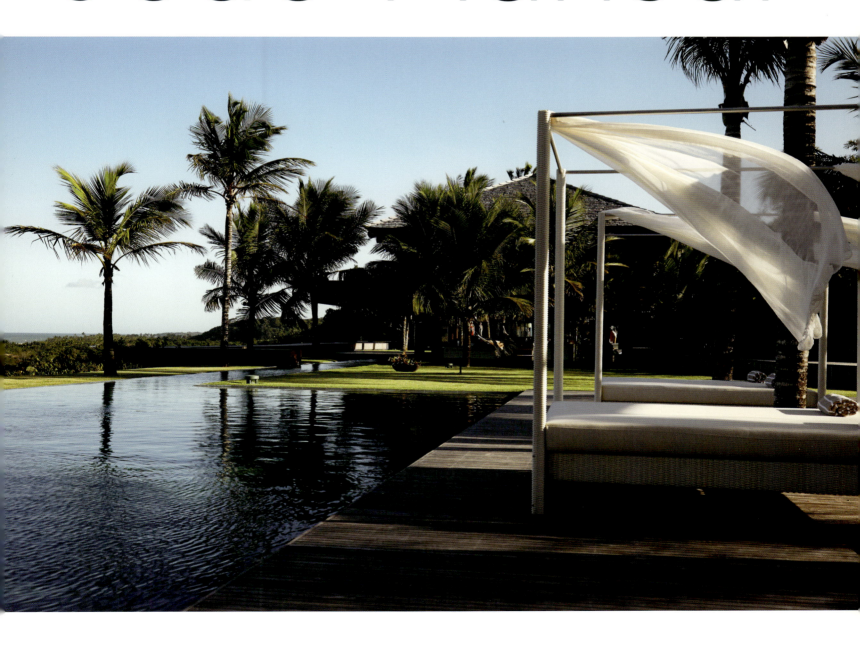

Designer: João Mansur. Company: João Mansur Arquitetura Design Arte, São Paulo, Brazil. Specialising in high end architectural projects, interior design and art consultancy in Brazil and overseas, including apartments, stores, restaurants, night clubs, hotels and offices. Current projects include the renovation of a 17th century building in Porto, Portugal to become a 'Hôtel Particulier', the refurbishment of a 50's Spanish style house in Coral Gables, Florida and a duplex apartment in front of the beach in Porto. Recent work includes the renovation of an apartment in Regent's Park, London. Design philosophy: timeless, custom made design, balancing classical with contemporary.

Bernd Gruber

Designer: Philipp Hoflehner. Company: Bernd Gruber, Kitzbühel, Austria. An international design brand specialising in luxury interior residential developments in Austria and overseas. Recent projects include the conversion of an apartment in Vienna and a chalet in Kirchberg. Forthcoming work includes three chalets in Switzerland, a city apartment in Bogenhausen, Munich and the reconstruction of a seaside apartment in Marbella, Spain. Design philosophy: beauty, individuality, humanity.

Greg Natale

Designer: Greg Natale. Company: Greg Natale Design, Sydney, Australia. Specialising in residential and commercial projects at home and abroad. Current work includes a large home in Oklahoma, the complete refurbishment of an 80 room luxury hotel in Australia's Hunter Valley, as well as a landmark Sydney Harbour waterfront home set over four floors. Recent work includes a world class horse stud in Victoria, an expansive compound-like residence in Brisbane as well as a large riverside family home in Sydney. Design philosophy: to fuse decoration and design, make precision look effortless, respect the classic and the contemporary.

Ruth Canning

Designer: Ruth Canning. Company: Canning & Sheridan, Essex, UK. Specialising in highly individual residential and boutique commercial projects primarily in London. Recent work includes the private members room at The Barbican Centre, a Docklands warehouse apartment and a family home. Design philosophy: to create comfortable, functional homes that express the clients' character.

Michael Clattenburg

Designer: Michael Clattenburg. Company: Michael Clattenburg Interiors L.L.C.; Dubai, United Arab Emirates. Specialising in residential interior design predominantly in Dubai but also internationally. Recent work includes two luxury residential projects in Dubai and a beach villa in Dibba. Current work includes adapting the interior architecture of a villa and the planning of a public majlis for a football enthusiast. Design philosophy: logical, functional, beautiful and elegant.

Elin Fossland

Designer: Elin Fossland. Company: ArkitektFossland AS, Drammen, Norway. Specialising in summer houses, mountain chalets, private residences and apartments as well as hotels and restaurants. Current work includes several chalets, a seaside house in Kragerø and a residence in Oslo. Recent projects include apartments in Geilo and Bergen and a large historic family home. Design philosophy: interiors should harmonise with the people who live in them.

Chen Yi & Zhang Muchen

Designers: Chen Yi & Zhang Munchen. Company: Beijing Fenghemuchen Space Design Centre, Beijing, China. Specialising in classic real estate, commercial projects, landscape and product design. Recent work includes a sales centre in Wuhan, a sales club in Yinchuan and the architectural and interior design of Blue Lake restaurant in Beijing. Design philosophy: poetic expression, spiritual design.

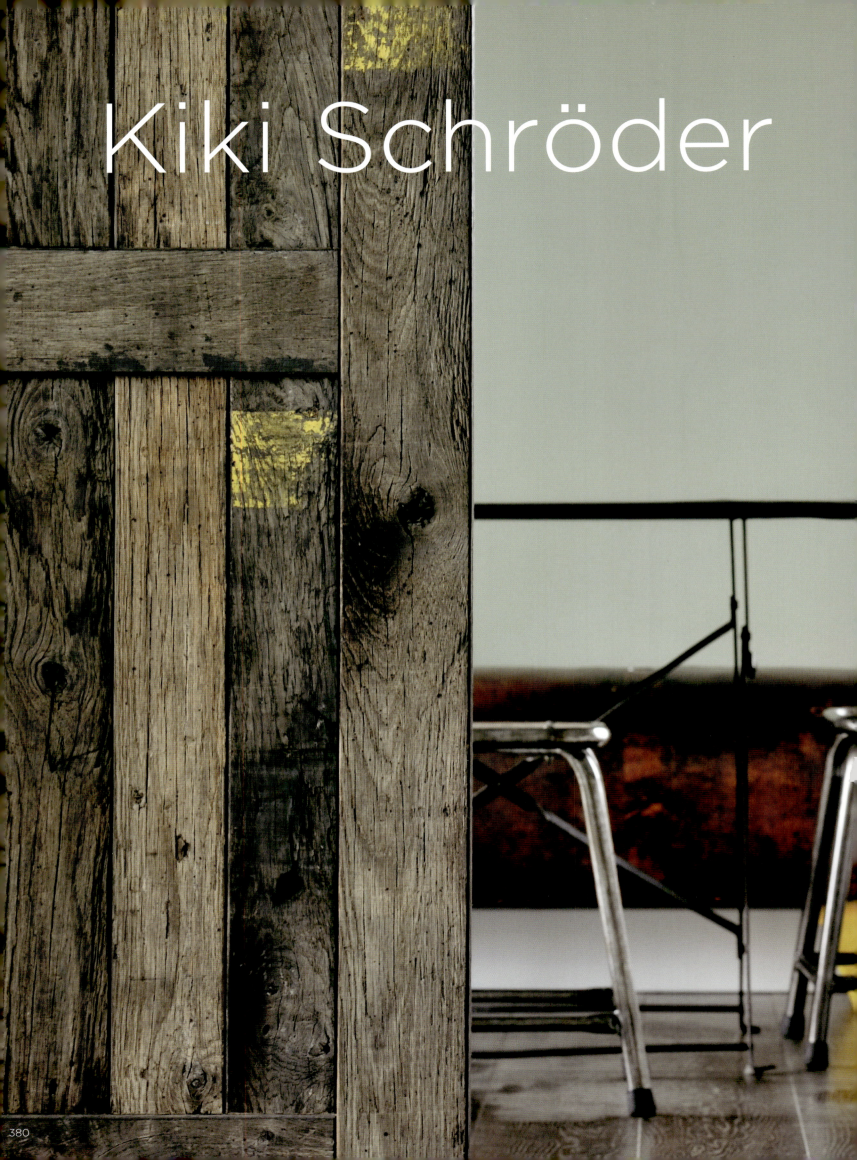

Kiki Schröder

Designer: Kiki Schröder. Company: Kiki Schröder Design GmbH, Hamburg, Germany. Specialising predominantly in high end residential and commercial space. Current projects include conceptual work for a medical company's headquarters in Berlin, the Hafen-Klub, Hamburg and a residential family home in Sylt. Recent work includes a large residential townhouse in Hamburg, a Käfer German kitchen and casual dining concept in The Hague and a residential family home in the North German countryside. Design philosophy: heart, soul and personality.

Bricks

Designer: James van der Velden. Company: BRICKS Amsterdam, The Netherlands. Specialising in commercial and residential projects in the Netherlands and overseas. Recent work includes a French Vietnamese restaurant and bar in Amsterdam, a large house in Amsterdam and The Thrill Grill burger bar in Haarlem. Recent projects include Brandbase head office in Amsterdam, a tailor's workshop in London and a school converted into a loft apartment. Design philosophy: eclectic, homely, surprising.

WELCOME TO
THRILL GRILL

FOR THE LOVE
OF BURGERS

THE CLASSIC BEEF
PULLED PORK THR
SKINNY THRILLER
BEEF THRILLER ME   NGE
SALMON THRILLER
VEGA THRILLER
CHICKEN THRILLER
SPICY BEEF THRIL
KRANENBURGER
CLASSIC HOT DOG
CHIEN CHAUD
WALDORF SALAD
POPCORN ICE CRE
YOGURT BASIL ICE
VANILLA MILKSHA
STRAWBERRY MIL

Designers in the City

Designers: Sonia Warner & Jacinta Woods. Company: Designers in the City, Sydney, Australia. Predominantly residential and boutique commercial projects. Current work includes a collection of contemporary apartments in the heart of the city, as well as several impressive family homes in the sought after areas of Sydney. Recent projects include the concept & project management of various homes on Sydney's North shore, whilst collaborating with a number of design teams to produce large scale residential projects in the Eastern Suburbs. Design philosophy: approachable, transparent, cohesive, flawless.

Zhou Wei

Designer: Zhou Wei. Company: ZW Architectural Design Institution, Hangzhou, China. Specialising in commercial space, including restaurants, boutique and resort hotels. Current projects include Mo Yi Tang boutique hotel, Ji Long Jian resort hotel and Ba Bei Long barbecue shop. Recent work includes Timed coffee shop, Mazin music restaurant and Peach hotel. Design philosophy: to give space a personality.

Christian's & Hennie

Designer: Helene Forbes Hennie. Company: Christian's & Hennie AS, Oslo, Norway. Projects are exclusive and international. Current work includes a mountain lodge in a Swedish ski resort, a hacienda in Spain and a family home in Oslo. Recent projects include a traditional, yet modern Asian restaurant, a private yacht and an Oslo townhouse. Design philosophy: elegant, comfortable and individual.

Studio Hertrich & Adnet

Designer: Marc Hertrich & Nicholas Adnet. Company: Studio Hertrich & Adnet, Paris, France. Specialising in luxury projects worldwide. Recent work includes Villa Diyafa boutique Hotel & Spa in the heart of Rabat, a Zen Pool, concept restaurant and kids club at Club Med Bali and the VIP lounges and shopping mall 'l'Avenue du Parc' at the Paris football stadium. Current projects include the renovation of Constance Lemuria Hotel in Praslin, Seychelles, Hotel Negresco in Nice and The Astor Hotel in Paris. Design philosophy: cultured, respectful, elegant.

Karl Weber

Designers: Karl Weber, Uli Kamolz-Weber, Thomas Kamolz. Company: Karl Weber Interior Design & Decoration, Zell am See, Austria. Specialising in residential projects, chalets and boutique hotels. Current work includes a luxury lakeside hotel in Austria, an apartment in Stuttgart and a family house in Vienna. Recent projects include a sea view villa in Sardinia, several private residences in Vienna, Salzburg and Kitzbühel and a primary residential project in Romania. Design philosophy: novelty, comfort and timelessness.

Designer: Ai Qing. Company: Qingtian Design, Beijing, China. Specialising in traditional Chinese courtyard houses, offices and commercial space. Recent projects include the office space of a 500 staff company in Shenyang, a lakeside hotel & shopping mall in Taiyuan and a Jiaxi tea house restaurant in Chongqing. Current work includes a boutique hotel in Wuling Mountain, a courtyard house in Beijing and the office space of a bank. Design philosophy: to pursue the beauty of life.

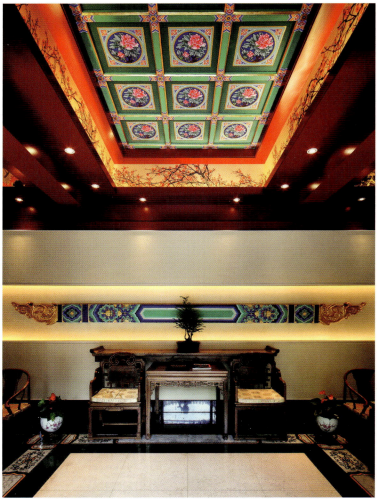

Qingtian Design

Jorge Cañete

Designer: Jorge Cañete. Company: Interior Design Philosophy, Saint-Saphorin-sur-Morges, Switzerland. High end interior design for private homes and corporate projects. Current work includes a house in Ortigia Siracusa, Philippa Smith's first solo art exhibition in Switzerland and a mansion in Geneva. Recent projects include an historic villa in Capri, a caravan in a tree-house resort and a therapist's office in Lausanne. Design philosophy: sensual alchemy, memory and modernity.

Toni Espuch

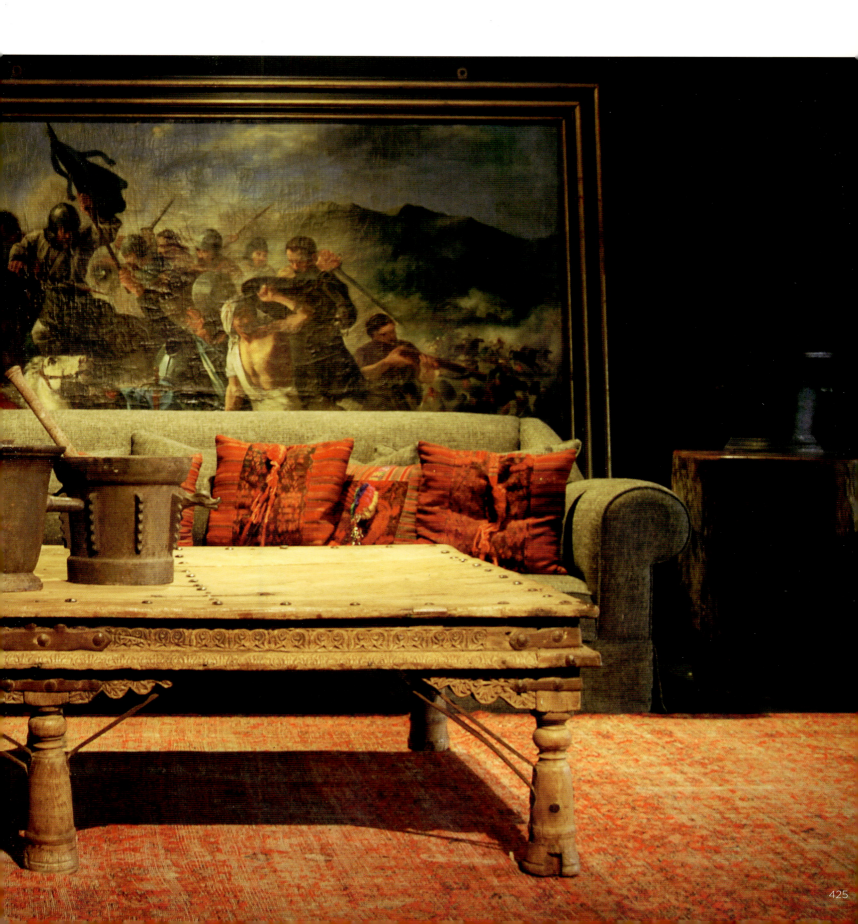

Designer: Toni Espuch. Company: AZULTIERRA, Barcelona, Spain. Specialising in luxury interior architecture worldwide. Projects are characterised by creating warm, intimate spaces. Current work includes a natural products showroom headquarters in Barcelona, the conversion of an old cinema into a restaurant in Madrid and a shop for a famous shoe brand inside the Mandarin Hotel. Recent projects include a luxury restaurant L'EGGS, DOBLE cocktail bar and a home in Barcelona. Design philosophy: to find beauty in imperfection.

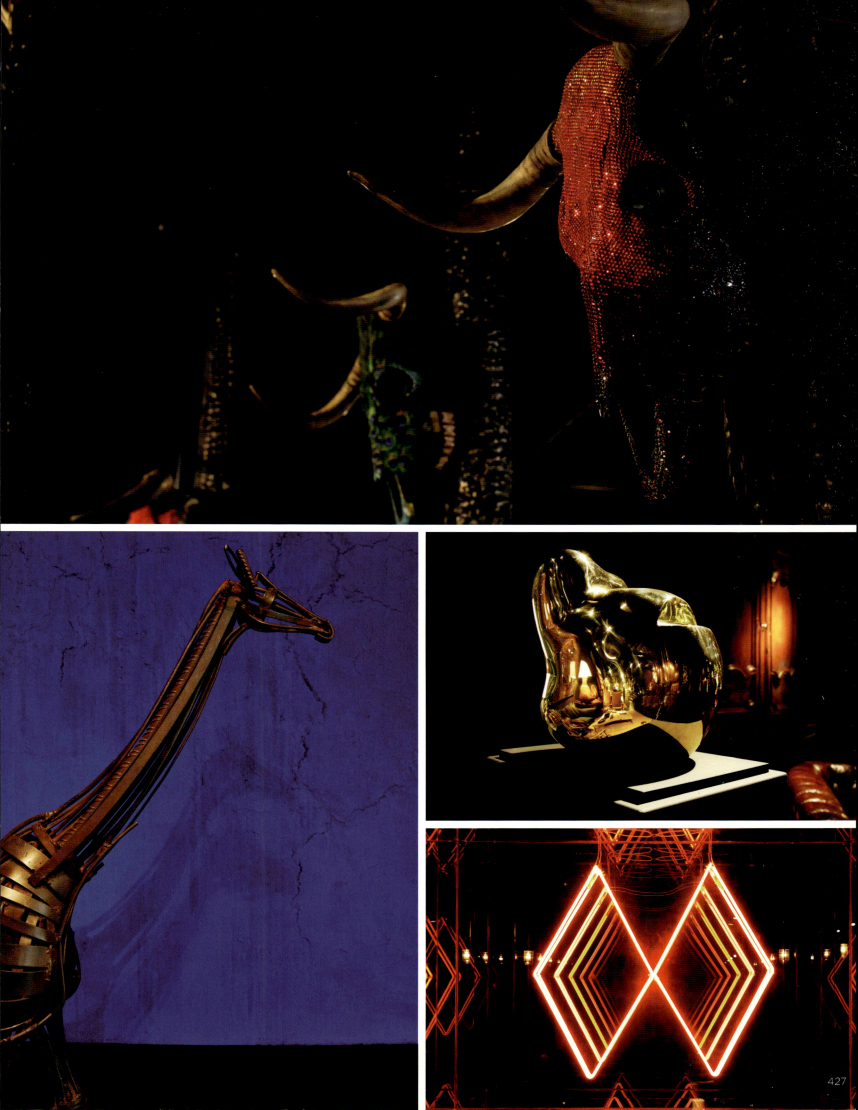

Designer: Irina Dymova. Irina Dymova Design Studio, Moscow, Russia. Specialising in luxury interior design. Recent projects include an apartment in London, two private villas in Ibiza, a spa in Mallorca and a luxurious office in central Moscow. Design philosophy: creative freedom.

Irina Dymova

Glamorous

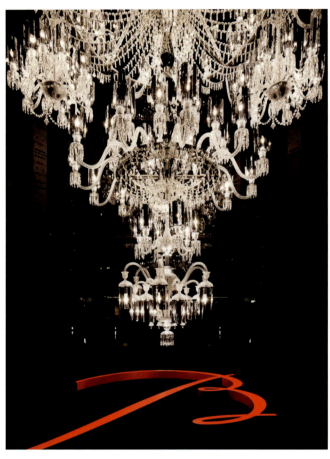 

Designer: Yasumichi Morita. Company: GLAMOROUS co.,ltd., Tokyo, Japan. Specialising in interior design in Japan and overseas including restaurants, bars, retail shops, offices, residences, spas and hotels. Recent projects include a restaurant in London, a clubhouse in Hong Kong and a 1,420 sq m office in Tokyo. Current work includes Isetan Shinjuku store, Iron Chef's restaurant Morimoto South Beach in Miami and Life is Flower, an artwork collaboration with Lladro. Design philosophy: bring happiness.

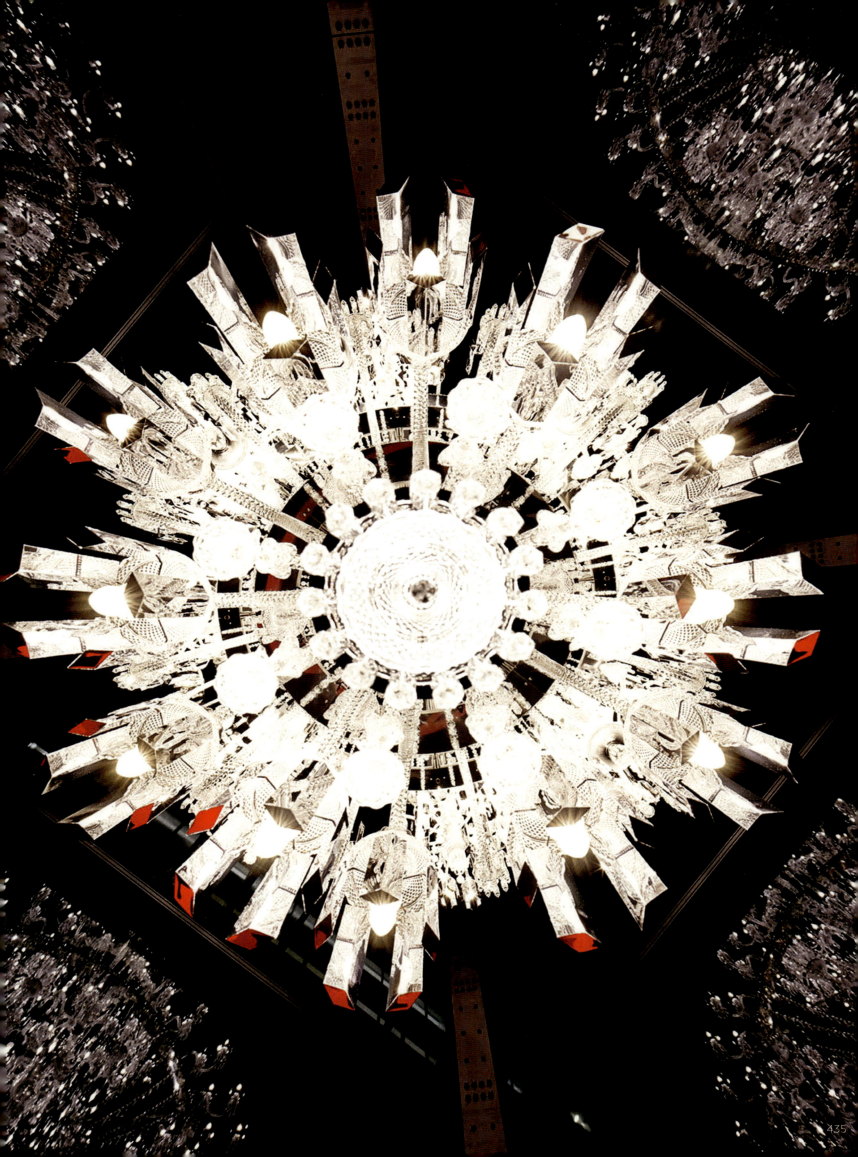

Staffan Tollgård

Designer: Staffan Tollgård. Company: Staffan Tollgård Design Group, London, UK. Specialising in creating bold, contemporary interiors in London and around the world. Current projects include villas in Amman and Riyadh, the refurbishment of a listed Belgravia home and the lateral conversion of listed apartments in Knightsbridge. Recent work includes listed buildings in Knightsbridge and Chelsea, an apartment in Hong Kong's Happy Valley and a villa in Southern California as well as an award winning rug collection for JAB Anstoetz and lighting for Contardi. Design philosophy: considered, contemporary, cultured.

Eye Interior

Designers: Sanna Nathanson & Ylva Ras. Company: Eye Interior, Stockholm, Sweden. Predominantly hospitality projects, residential and restaurants. Current work includes a boutique hotel in Stockholm, a country house and a luxury hotel in Norway. Recent projects include hotels in Stockholm, Germany and Southern Europe. Design philosophy: authentic, easy on the eye.

Designer: Laura Brucco. Company: Laura Brucco, Buenos Aires, Argentina. Specialising in luxury residential, commercial and corporate interiors. Recent work includes a flat in Miami Beach, a villa in a golf and polo club and several flats in the residential district of Buenos Aires. Current projects include several villas and various luxury family residences in the city. Design philosophy: timeless elegance.

Laura Brucco

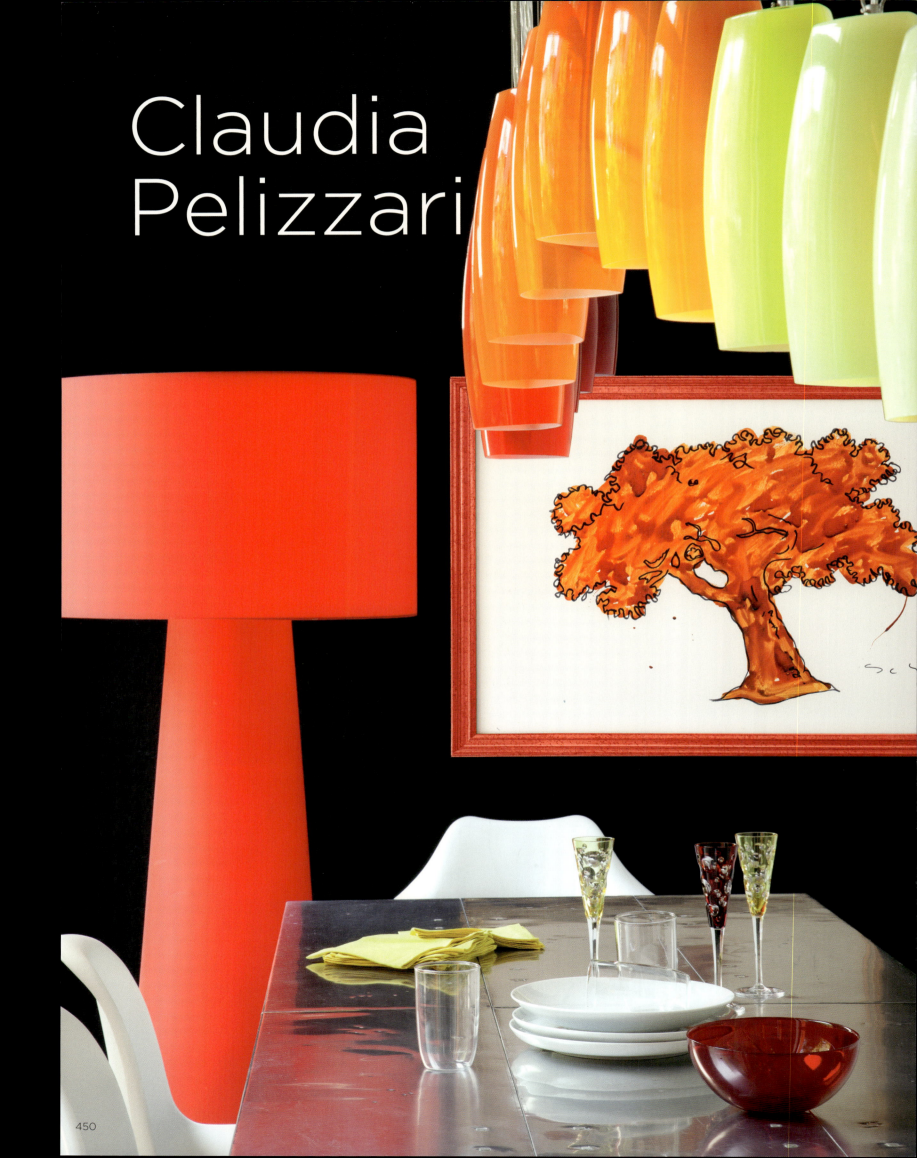

Claudia Pelizzari

Designer: Claudia Pelizzari. Company: Claudia Pelizzari Interior Design, Brescia, Italy. Specialising in luxury interior design, private homes, residential developments and boutique hotels in Italy, the French Riviera, Russia and Mongolia. Recent work includes the renovation of a 17th century palace in Northern Italy, a villa situated between Milan and Venice for an art collector and the renovation of a fashion store. Design philosophy: luxurious materials, human sensibility.

Shalini Misra

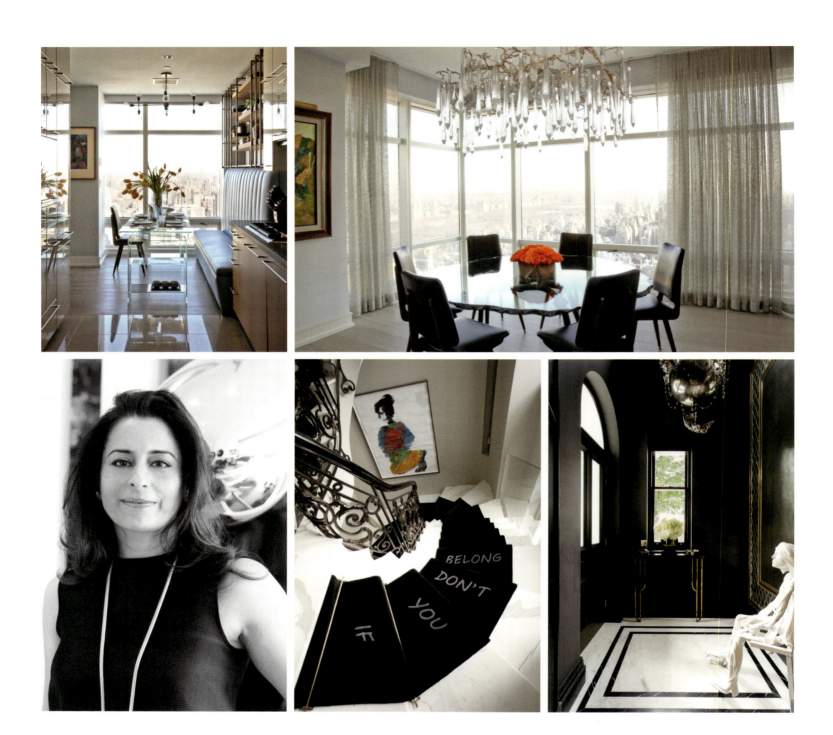

Designer: Shalini Misra. Company: Shalini Misra Ltd, London, UK. Specialising in bespoke interior architecture worldwide. Current projects include refurbishing a large family villa in Dubai, the architecture, interior and landscaping of a 20,000 sq ft new build country house in New Delhi and the remodelling and refurbishment of a period house in central London. Recent projects include the refurbishment of a 38th floor apartment in New York, the renovation of a seven bedroom home in Chelsea, London and the design and build of two penthouses in the air space above two Victorian buildings opposite Regent's Park, London. Design philosophy: holistic interiors that tell a story.

Designers: Raymond Jimenez & Shannon Scott. Company: RS3|DESIGNS, Florida, USA. Specialising in luxury, commercial and residential interior design in the US and overseas. Current projects include a 20,000 sq ft penthouse at the Ritz Carlton in Ft. Lauderdale, a boutique lobby and common areas in Midtown Miami with 30,000 sq ft pool deck and a Grand Estate residence in Coconut Grove, Florida. Recent work includes private residences in high rise condominiums in South Florida, such as Murano Portofino, Point of Americas II and St. Regis. Other works include exterior renovations of entrances, pool decks and exterior common areas for Bristol Tower in Brickell, Fl and L'Hermitage in Ft. Lauderdale. Design philosophy: think different, design different.

RS3 | DESIGNS

Design
Intervention

Designers: Nikki Hunt & Andrea Savage. Company: Design Intervention, Singapore. A multi award winning studio specialising in luxury and boutique commercial projects. Current work includes a mountain resort in Japan, a private family complex in Singapore and

an Indonesian Island resort. Recent projects include a townhouse complex in Niseko, Japan, an elegant Singapore penthouse and a family mansion in Malaysia. Design philosophy: to create bespoke interiors with personality.

RPW Design

Designers: Jan Wilson & Elizabeth Lane. Company: RPW Design, London, UK. A specialist interior design consultancy with over 25 years experience. Current work includes the extensive renovation of a Grade II* listed 5 star hotel in central London, the creation of the interiors for a new 5 star hotel

in Nigeria as well as a luxury beach resort in Ibiza. Recently completed projects include the Marriott Hotel Park Lane in London, the Hotel Continental in Oslo and Mayfair's exclusive gaming club, Crockfords. Design philosophy: to create coherent, individual and elegant interiors.

Trenzseater

Designers: Ben & Hamish Lewis, TRENZSEATER, Christchurch & Auckland, New Zealand. Specialising in luxury residential and commercial interior design projects both in New Zealand and internationally. Current work includes several properties in both Auckland and Christchurch, a substantial hillside home as well as an exclusive office building also in Christchurch and a holiday home in Queenstown. Recent projects include prestigious apartments in Auckland, Christchurch and Queenstown plus several high end private residences and holiday homes. Design philosophy: grand, distinct, sophisticated, opulent.

Keech Green

Designer: Graham Green and Michael Keech. Company: Keech Green, London, UK. Specialising in luxury residential developments in the UK and overseas. Current projects include a penthouse apartment in Monaco, two substantial coastal villas in Italy and a large country house in Germany. Recent work includes a house in Moscow and apartments in Mayfair and Geneva. Design philosophy: to create classic and timeless interiors which fully realise the clients' brief.

VESNA-LETO

Designers: Anna Smirnova & Yulian Suetin. Company: VESNA-LETO Interior Studio, Moscow, Russia. Specialising in private homes and boutique shops in Russia and overseas. Current projects include an apartment, a gastronomic boutique and the lobby of a private building, all in Moscow. Recent work includes a house in Zarechye and a loft in Skolkovo. Design philosophy: to create the space between reality and fiction, dreams and awake, past and future, life and cinema.

Rung-Lu Liou

Designer: Rung-Lu Liou. Company: Very Space International, Taipei, Taiwan. Specialising in award winning space planning and experimental exhibition design. Current projects include villas in Xinyi District, apartments in Da-an District and apartments in Zhonghe District all in Taipei. Recent work includes Zhongshan Liu's Mansion, Exhibition Space, Yiping Huang's Mansion, Residential space, Taiyuan City and Yungyi's 12F offices, Xinyi District, Taipei City. Design philosophy: spiritual, aesthetic, ground breaking.

Alessandra Branca

Designer: Alessandra Branca. Company: Branca, Inc. Chicago, USA. An international design firm that specialises in residential, commercial and hospitality design. Current projects include apartments in New York and Chicago and a farmhouse in Michigan. Recent work includes an apartment in Rome, a hotel in Harbour Island and a penthouse apartment in Chicago. Design philosophy: fuse old world craftsmanship with energy and practicality.

Clearspace

Designer: Ryan Kuo. Company: Clearspace Design & Research, Taiwan. Predominantly residential and commercial projects including villas, salons, shops, spas, dental clinics and public artwork. Current projects include a villa in Taipei and the renovation of a house and an apartment. Recent work includes apartments in Taoyung and a five storey family home in Northern Taiwan. Design philosophy: ecology, contemporary art, fashion, humanist.

Designer: Steve Leung. Company: Steve Leung Designers, Hong Kong, China. Consisting of a team of 400 staff specialising in residential, commercial and hospitality design projects. Recent work includes Double Cove in Hong Kong, Mandarin Palace in Nanjing and Great Taipei New Town in Taipei. Current projects include 8 Conlay in Kuala Lumpur, an apartment project in Tokyo and Ping An International Finance Centre in Shenzhen. Design philosophy: design without limits.

Steve Leung

272 Douglas Mackie
D Mackie Design
123-125 Gloucester Place
London W1U 6JZ
Tel: +44 207 487 3295
douglas@dmackiedesign.com
www.dmackiedesign.com

276 Rosa May Sampaio
Rua Alemanha, 691 - Jd. Europa
São Paulo
Brazil. CEP 01448 010
Tel: +55 (11) 3085 7100
rosamaysampaio@terra.com.br
www.rosamaysampaio.com.br

280 Ryu Kosaka
A.N.D. (NOMURA Co. Ltd)
Qiz Aoyama 3F
3-39-5 Jingumae
Shibuya-ku, Tokyo
150- 0001 Japan
Tel: +81 3 5412 6785
Fax: +81 3 3479 8050
ky.iwata@nomura-g.jp
www.and-design.jp

286 Richard Ouellette
Les Ensembliers
1604 Notre-Dame Ouest
Montréal, Québec
H3J 1M1 Canada
Tel: +514 938 4424
info@ensembliers.com
www.ensembliers.com

290 Heidi Meyer
Yohm Studio
24 Box Street, Buderim
Queensland 4556
Australia
Tel: +61 (0) 4103 64542
heidi@yohm.com.au
www.yohm.com.au

296 LH Chan
TDC & Associates Pte Ltd
3791 Jalan Bukit Merah
#09-01 E-Centre, @Redhill
Singapore 159471
Tel: +65 6295 6883
mail@tdc.com.sg
www.tdc.com.sg

300 Mark Rielly, Jon Case
& Michele Rhoda
ARRCC
109 Hatfield Street
Gardens
Cape Town 8001 South Africa.
info@arrcc.com
www.arrcc.com

306 Chang Ching-Ping
Tien Fun Interior Planning Co Ltd
12F No 211 Chung Min Road
North District
Taichung, City 404
Taiwan
Tel: +886 4 220 18908
tf@mail.tienfun.tw
www.tienfun.com.tw

312 Pamela Makin
Les Interieurs
104 Glenmore Road, Paddington
NSW Australia
Tel: + 40 850 0400
pamela@lesinterieurs.com.au
www.lesinterieurs.com.au

318 Kris Lin
KLID, Floor 3
Building 4, Lane 1163
Hongqiao Road
Shanghai
China
Tel: +86 21 620 999 18
krislindesign@vip.163.com
www.krislin.com.cn

322 Francisco Neves
5 Janelas Interior Design
Av. D. Afonso Henriques 740
4810-431 Guimarães
Portugal
Tel: +351 253 516 155
5janelas@gmail.com
www.5janelas.com

328 Angelos Angelopoulos.
ANGELOS ANGELOPOULOS
5 Frynonos Street
116 36 Athens
Greece
Tel: +30 210 756 7191
Fax: +30 210 756 7191
design@angelosangelopoulos.com
www.angelosangelopoulos.com

334 Flora Lau
Flora Lau Designers Ltd
Unit D, 10/F
Hoi Bun Industrial Building
6 Wing Yip Street, Kwun Tong,
Kowloon, Hong Kong
Tel: +852 2893 8007
Fax: +852 2893 8067
info@fldesigners.com.hk
www.fldesigners.com.hk

338 Nastya Komarova
Garibaldi 36-344
Moscow 117418 Russia
Tel: +8499 718 2238
inside@nastyakomarova.com
www.nastyakomarova.com

344 Joao Mansur
Joao Mansur Arquitetura Design Arte
1922b Rua Groenlândia
Jardim America, São Paulo
SP, Brazil
Tel: +55 11 3083 1500
joaomansur@joaomansur.com
www.joaomansur.com

348 Philipp Hoflehner
Bernd Gruber GmbH
Pass-Thurn-Stasse 8
6371 Kitzbühel, Austria
Tel: +43 5356 711 01
atelier@bernd-gruber.at
www.berndtgruber.at

354 Greg Natale
Greg Natale Design
62 Buckingham St, Surry Hills
Sydney 2030 NSW Australia
Tel: +61 (0) 2 8399 2103
info@gregnatale.com
www.gregnatale.com

362 Ruth Canning
Canning & Sheridan
13 The Clock Tower
The Galleries
Brentwood CM14 5GF
Tel: +44 (0) 7884 182 811
info@canningsheridan.com
www.canningsheridan.com

366 Michael Clattenburg
Michael Clattenburg Interiors LLC
P.O. Box 49235
Dubai, UAE.
& P.O. Box 547
114 11 Stockholm, Sweden.
info@michaelclattenburg.com
www.michaelclattenburg.com

370 Elin Fossland.
ARKITEKTFOSSLAND AS
Kirkegata 8
3016 Drammen, Norway
PO Box 275 Bragernes
3001 Drammen
Norway
Tel: +47 916 64 684
elin@arkitektfossland.no
www.arkitektfossland.no

376 Yi Chen & Muchen Zhang
Beijing Fenghemuchen Space Design
4-B-1402 Bai zi wan
Hou Xian Dai Cheng
Chaoyang District
Beijing, China 100024
Tel: +10-87732690
Fax: +10-87765176
fenghemuchen@163.com
www.fenghemuchen.com

380 Kiki Schroeder
Kiki Schroeder Design
Grindelhof 81
20146 Hamburg
Germany
Tel: +49 40 41 62 27 30
info@kikischroeder-design.de
www.kikischroeder-design.de

386 James van der Velden
BRICKS Amsterdam
Eerste passeerdersdwarsstraat 74,
1016 XD Amsterdam
The Netherlands
Tel: +31 (0) 20 320 4388
info@bricks-amsterdam.com
www.bricksamsterdam.com

390 Sonia Warner & Jacinta Woods
Designers in the City
330b Miller Street
Cammeray
NSW 2062 Australia
Tel: +61 9954 4901
info@designersinthecity.com.au
www.designersinthecity.com.au

396 Zhou Wei
ZW Architectural Design Institution
49 Tong Yi Road
Hang Zhou
China
Tel:+8657186166769

402 Helene Hennie
CHRISTIAN'S & HENNIE AS
Skovveien 6
0257 Oslo, Norway
Tel: +47 22 12 13 50
Fax: +47 22 12 13 51
info@christiansoghennie.no
www.christiansoghennie.no

408 Marc Hertrich & Nicolas Adnet
Studio Hertrich & Adnet
(Studio MHNA SAS)
5 Passage Piver, 75011 Paris
France
Tel: +33 1 43 14 00 00
Fax: +33 1 43 38 86 01
contact@studiomhna.com
www.studiomhna.com

412 Karl Weber
Karl Weber Interior Design
& Decoration
Anton Wallner Str. 11-13
A-5700 Zell am See
Austria
Tel: +43 6542 722 330
thomas@weber-deco.com
info@weber-deco.com
www.weber-deco.com

416 Ai Qing
Qing Tian Design
A-2b
Jinyuan Times Commercial Centre
Yuanda Road
Beijing, China
Tel: +86 10 88 86 17 50
info@quingtian-art.com
www.qingtian-design.com

420 Jorge Canete
Interior Design Philosophy
Le Pavé 2
Chateau de Saint-Saphorin sur
Morges, CH-1113
Saint- Saphorin sur Morges
Switzerland
Tel: +41 787 102 534
info@jorgecanete.com
www.jorgecanete.com

424 Toni Espuch
AZULTIERRA
C/Córcega 276-282
08008 Barcelona, Spain
Tel/Fax: +34 932 178 356
azultierra@azultierra.es
www.azultierra.es

430 Irina Dymova
Irina Dymova Design Studio
30/12 Shabolovka Str
Apartment
114 Moscow, 115419 Russia
Tel: +7 (495) 953 9863
dymovadecor@yandex.ru

434 Yasumichi Morita
Glamorous co ltd
2F, 2-7-25 Motoazabu
Minato-Ku
Tokyo 106 0046 Japan
Tel: +81 3 5475 1037
info@glamorous.co.jp
www.glamorous.co.jp

438 Staffan Tollgard
Staffan Tollgard Design Group
Gatliff Road
Grosvenor Waterside
London, SW1W 8QN, UK
Tel: +44 20 7952 6066
info@tollgard.co.uk
www.tollgard.co.uk

442 Sanna Nathanson
Eye Interior
Birger Jarlsgatan 104
114 20 Stockholm
Sweden
Tel: +46 708 15 80 92
studio@eyeinterior.com
www.eyeinterior.com

446 Laura Brucco
Castex 3228 PB - C1425CDC
Buenos Aires
Argentina
Tel: +5411 4808 9565
Mobile: +549 4448 2120
laurabrucco@gmail.com
www.laurabrucco.com

450 Claudia Pelizzari
Claudia Pelizzari Interior Design
Corso Matteotti, 54
25122 Brescia, Italy
Tel: +39 030 2900 088
info@pelizzari.com
www.pelizzari.com

456 Shalini Misra
Shalini Misra Ltd
4b Lonsdale Road
London NW6 6RD
Tel: +44 207 604 2340
info@shalinimisra.com
www.shalinimisra.com

460 Raymond Jimenez
& Shannon Scott
RS3|DESIGNS
MIAMI DESIGN DISTRICT
1 NE 40th ST MIAMI,
FL 33137 STE. 103, USA
Tel: +786-310-7324
info@rs3designs.com
www.rs3designs.com

464 Nikki Hunt & Andrea Savage
Design Intervention
75E Loewen Road
Singapore 248845
Tel: +65 6506 0920
Fax: +65 6468 7418
www.designintervention.com.sg

470 Jan Wilson
RPW Design
124 Aldersgate Street
London EC1A 4JQ
Tel: +44 207 780 7277
rpw@rpwdesign.co.uk
www.rpwdesign.co.uk

476 Ben Lewis
TRENZSEATER
121 Blenheim Road, Christchurch 8041
New Zealand
Tel: +64 3 343 0876
& 80 Parnell Road, Parnell
Auckland 1052, New Zealand
Tel: +64 9 303 4151
benlewis@trenzseater.com
www.trenzseater.com

480 Graham Green & Michael Keech
Keech Green
414 Chambers East
The Design Centre Chelsea Harbour
London SW10 OXF
Tel: +44 20 7351 5701
graham@keechgreen.com
www.keechgreen.com

484 Anna Smirnova & Yulian Suetin
VESNA-LETO Interior Studio
Kozhevnicheskaya Ulitsa 5
115114 Moscow, Russia
Tel: +7 926 221 9107 & +7 926 850 2344
vesna-leto.info@yandex.ru
www.vesna-leto.org

488 Rung-Lu Liou
Very Space International
11F, No. 17, Sec. 5
Chung-Hsiao E. Rd.
Taipei, Taiwan 110
Tel: +886 2 2749 1238
id@very-space.com
www.very-space.com

494 Alessandra Branca
Branca
5 East Goethe Street, Chicago
IL 60610 USA
Tel: +312 787 6123
& 9 East 68th St, New York NY 10065
Tel: +212 257 640
info@branca.com
www.branca.com

500 Ryan Kuo
ClearSpace Architecture and
Interior Design
No. 205-1, Wuzu St., Jhongli City
Taoyuan 32045, Taiwan
Tel: +886 3 281 3777
Fax: 886 3 281 2900
info@clearspace.tw
kuoshai@gmail.com
www.clearspace.tw

504 Steve Leung
Steve Leung Designers Ltd
30/F Manhattan Place
23 Wang Tai Road
Kowloon Bay, Hong Kong
Tel: +852 2527 1600
Fax: +852 3549 8398
sld@steveleung.com
www.steveleung.com

Editor Martin Waller
Project Executive Annika Bowman
Design by Graphicom Design

teNeues Publishing Group
Kempen
Berlin
London
Munich
New York
Paris

Production by Nele Jansen, teNeues Media
Editorial coordination Stephanie Rebel, teNeues Media
Colour separation by SPM Print

First published in 2015 by teNeues Media GmbH & Co. KG, Kempen

teNeues Media GmbH & Co. KG
Am Selder 37, 47906 Kempen, Germany
Phone: +49-(0)2152-916-0
Fax: +49-(0)2152-916-111
e-mail: books@teneues.com

teNeues Publishing Company
7 West 18th Street, New York, NY 10011, USA
Phone: +1-212-627-9090
Fax: +1-212-627-9511

Press department: Andrea Rehn
Phone: +49-(0)2152-916-202
e-mail: arehn@teneues.com

teNeues Publishing UK Ltd.
12 Ferndene Road, London SE24 0AQ, UK
Phone: +44-(0)20-3542-8997

teNeues France S.A.R.L
39, rue des Billets, 18250 Henrichemont, France
Phone: +33-(0)2-4826-9348
Fax: +33-(0)1-7072-3482

www.teneues.com

ISBN 978-3-8327-3271-4
Printed in The Czech Republic

FSC MIX
Papier aus verantwortungsvollen Quellen
Paper from responsible sources
FSC® C005833
www.fsc.org

Bibliographic information published by the Deutsche Nationalbibliothek.
The Deutsche Nationalbibliothek lists this publication in the Deutsche Nationalbibliografie; detailed bibliographic data are available in the Internet at http://dnb.d-nb.de.

Acknowledgments

The author and publisher wish to thank all the owners and designers of the projects featured in this book.

They also thank the following photographers:

Matthew Millman, Tubay Yabut, Mel Yates, Chen Wei Zhong, Jenni Hare, Wu Hui, Giorgio Baroni, Simon Brown, Andrew Beasley, Aleksandra Laska, Giorgio Possenti, Thierry Malty, Raymond Tam, Zacandzac, Patrick Berlan, Jo Pauwels, Allan Hayslip, Danny Piassick, David Duncan Livingston, Edina Van der Wyck, Julian Abrams, Srdjan Milinkovic, Ulso Tsang, Maria Bastos Vasconcelos, Eric Roth, Montse Garriga Grau, Carlos Vasconcelos e Sa, Michael Calderwood, Bruno Barbosa, Fram Petit, Sebastian Zachariah, Jonathan Leijonhufvud, Edmon Leong, Debra Cronin, Ali Bekman, Mustafa Nurdogdu, Sergio Ghetti, Kerem Sanlıman, Ed Reeves, Mack Liang, Yurii Molodkovetz, Ray Main, Anson Smart, Matt Livey, Philip Durrant, Mike Caldwell, Nick Guttridge, Alex Allwood, Lou, Kwou-Chi, Elsa Young, Frank Features, Sargent Architectural Photography, Brian McKee, Krishna Adithya, Pedro Goncalves – Servifoto, Francisco Almeida Dias, Alexandra Schauer, Chishou Wang, Chihcheng Chao, Jeffrey Allen, Jon Day, Costas Picadas, Martin Pope, Tim Beddow, Adam Letch, Ragnar Hartvig, Sharyn Cairns, Simon Whitbread, Simon Upton, Romulo Fialdini, Nacasa & Partners, Andre Rider, Jaimi Kenny, TDC & Associates, Lorenzo Vecchia, Adam Letch, Ching-Ping Chang, Felix Forest, KLID, Miguel Oliveira, Eddie Chan, Mihail Stepanov, Salvador Cordaro, Thomas Popinger, Ruth Canning, Hameed Ahmad Abbas, Stig-Goran Nilsson, Mona Gundersen, Xiang yu Sun, Zhiyi Zhou, Jens Bruchhaus, Oliver Heinemann, BRICKS, Tom Ferguson, Anneke Hill, Jia Fang, Mona Gundersen, Rupert Peace, Clare Booth, Alan Keohane, Fabrice Coiffard, Choukia MG, Serge Detalle, Robert Kovacs, Antoine Baralhé, Daniel Driessler, Zhang Qilin, Gaelle Le Boulicaut, Desiree Quagliara, Joan Guillamat, Vicente Nebot, Irina Dymova, I Susa, Richard Gooding, Magnus Marding, Jason Strong, Thomas Wingstedt, Christopher Dracke, Daniela Mac Adden, Giorgio Baroni, Tom Sullam, Amit Mehra, Barry Grossman, Joann Gamelo, RPW Design, Jim Ellan, Hotel Continental Oslo, London Marriot Hotel Park Lane, Hamish Lewis, Jamie McGregor Smith, Mikhail Stepanov, Will Webster, Kuo-Min Li, Douglas Friedman, Kana Okada, Kyle Yu, Mr Chen Zhong.